Discovering Christ the Servant

DISCOVERING CHRIST THE SERVANT

A SPIRITUALITY OF SERVICE

Deacon Dominic Cerrato, Ph.D.
Foreword by Deacon Harold Burke-Sivers

Our Sunday Visitor
Huntington, Indiana

Nihil Obstat
Msgr. Michael Heintz, Ph.D.
Censor Librorum

Imprimatur
✠ Kevin C. Rhoades
Bishop of Fort Wayne-South Bend
November 19, 2021

The *Nihil Obstat* and *Imprimatur* are official declarations that a book is free from doctrinal or moral error. It is not implied that those who have granted the *Nihil Obstat* and *Imprimatur* agree with the contents, opinions, or statements expressed.

Except where noted, the Scripture citations used in this work are taken from the *New American Bible, revised edition* © 2010, 1991, 1986, 1970 Confraternity of Christian Doctrine, Washington, D.C., and are used by permission of the copyright owner. All rights reserved. No part of the *New American Bible* may be reproduced in any form without permission in writing from the copyright owner.

English translation of the Catechism of the Catholic Church for use in the United States of America copyright © 1994, United States Catholic Conference, Inc. — Libreria Editrice Vaticana. English translation of the Catechism of the Catholic Church: Modifications from the Editio Typica copyright © 1997, United States Catholic Conference, Inc. — Libreria Editrice Vaticana.

Every reasonable effort has been made to determine copyright holders of excerpted materials and to secure permissions as needed. If any copyrighted materials have been inadvertently used in this work without proper credit being given in one form or another, please notify Our Sunday Visitor in writing so that future printings of this work may be corrected accordingly.

Copyright © 2022 by Deacon Dominic Cerrato, Ph.D.

27 26 25 24 23 22   1 2 3 4 5 6 7 8 9

All rights reserved. With the exception of short excerpts for critical reviews, no part of this work may be reproduced or transmitted in any form or by any means whatsoever without permission from the publisher. For more information, visit: www.osv.com/permissions.

Our Sunday Visitor Publishing Division

Our Sunday Visitor, Inc., 200 Noll Plaza, Huntington, IN 46750
www.osv.com 1-800-348-2440
ISBN: 978-1-68192-783-1 (Inventory No. T2652)
RELIGION—Christian Ministry—General.
RELIGION—Christian Living—Spiritual Growth.
RELIGION—Christianity—Catholic.

eISBN: 978-1-68192-784-8
LCCN: 2022930158
Cover and Interior design: Amanda Falk
Cover art: © Musée Condé, Chantilly / Bridgeman Images
Interior art: Renata Sedmakova / Shutterstock.com, AdobeStock

PRINTED IN THE UNITED STATES OF AMERICA

*Dedicated to the laity who seek
to follow Christ the Servant*

Contents

Foreword *by Deacon Harold Burke-Sivers*   9

Introduction: The Search for Intimacy   13
    Beginning the Journey   22
    Internalizing a Servant Spirituality   29
    Meditations and Reflections   33

Chapter One: A Spirituality Rooted in the Diaconate   37
    Toward a Clearer Understanding of Service   41
    The Origins of Holy Orders   44
    Establishment and Institution   60
    Relationship, Identity, and Mission   63
    Putting It All Together   71
    Meditations and Reflections   73

Chapter Two: The Centrality of the Spiritual Life   77
    The Interior Life as a Place of Encounter   79
    The Distinctiveness of a Spirituality of Service   83
    The Importance of Empathy   86
    Struggle in the Spiritual Life   89
    The Unholy Trinity and Sloth   90
    Grace as a Remedy   95
    Surrender Is Abandonment   96
    Struggle as a Way of Perfection   98
    Meditations and Reflections   105

Chapter Three: The Necessity of Surrender   109
    Awareness of the Ever-Present God   114
    God's Hidden Operations   118
    The Sacrament of the Present Moment   124
    Meditations and Reflections   129

Chapter Four: The Servant Mysteries   133
    Characteristics of the Servant Mysteries   134
    A Beauty That Wounds   141
    Keeping the Wounds Open   147
    Applying the Sacrament of the Present
       Moment   151
    Prayer of Abandonment and Little Examen   154
    Morning Prayer of Abandonment   156
    Little Examen   158
    Meditations and Reflections   159

Final Thoughts   163
Notes   167

Foreword

Following the recommendation of the Second Vatican Council, Pope St. Paul VI restored the diaconate as a permanent order in 1967. In his mandate the pope listed among the duties of deacons "to promote and sustain the apostolic activities of laymen." The deacon, in the Council's mind, was to support and encourage lay ministers by helping to develop their talents.

However, in the ensuing years since Vatican II, there has been a steady tension between deacons and lay persons. Sadly, this tension has manifested itself particularly within the ministry of service to the Church, both inside and outside the parish. You may hear, for example, comments from a volunteer who says, "the deacon and I are both serving the poor, what's the difference?" or "Except for serving at the altar, I can do everything a deacon does for the Church." Much of this stems from a poor understanding of what it means to serve as a deacon and as a lay person.

In *Discovering Christ the Servant,* Deacon Cerrato has provided a concise yet detailed spiritual roadmap leading to a deeper understanding of lay service. What surprised me was his approach: developing a lay spirituality of service by looking through the lens of diaconal service. Absolutely brilliant! In this way, Deacon Cerrato has helped ease the tension between deacons and laity in a way that has never been done before.

This book is much more than a comparison of ministerial service between laity and deacons. It speaks to the realities of the spiritual journey as all of us — lay or ordained — work to deepen our intimacy with the Lord in the midst of life's busyness and challenges. The spiritual life is about seeking the face of the Lord and yearning for Him, listening to the Master's precepts and inclining the ear of our hearts, and uniting our hearts more closely to the Lord's most Sacred Heart. This "entails a lifelong process" that "requires a certain death-to-self, a willingness to let go and allow God to enter more deeply into their lives." This integrated, holistic approach to discovering Christ the servant as a lay person unites prayer, theology, and worship.

Jesus teaches that his Father in heaven gives each person talents according to His will, and we are to use our gifts to glorify God. Our Lord has given us an immeasurable gift: the ability, through grace, to share in His life. At the cost of His own life, the Savior of the world has entrusted His greatest possession to those He has redeemed. Deacons and laity must work together, each with our unique gifts of service, to participate in Christ's mission by manifesting God's love to the world.

Saint John tells us: "If we love one another, God remains in us, and his love is brought to perfection in us.... God is love, and whoever in love remains in God and God in him" (1 Jn 4:12, 16). This is the foundational center of Deacon Cerrato's approach to lay service: The Father's love is so great, so powerful, and so real that He cannot keep it to Himself. God created us so that we can experience and participate in that love. Through Christ and in the Holy Spirit, the Father reaches out to deacon and lay person in love and invites us into a relationship of loving and life-giving communion.

Our being united in God's love leads us to serve. God the Father did not hold back His love when He created us; God the Son did not hold back His love on the cross; God the Holy Spirit did not hold back His love on Pentecost. Therefore, God expects us to do the same — to make a gift of ourselves to others in love, holding nothing back. This is the heart of service! *Discovering Christ the Servant* will help lay ministers recognize that every person, no matter who they are and what talents they have been given by God, has something to offer. The reader will discover that "deacons can share their spirituality with the laity, emboldening them to discover Christ the Servant anew and, in doing so, draw closer to Him. It will also have the secondary effect of catechizing the laity on the diaconate."

Our example of self-giving, self-sacrificing love is the cross of Jesus Christ. Jesus came to transform the culture with His truth and love, and if we *truly* want to be His disciples, we must pray daily for a love that casts out all fear so that we may become children of the light. Deacon Cerrato draws from the timeless wellspring of Holy Scripture, Sacred Tradition, and the saints in a way that — when combined with his own thoughtful, Christ-centered insights into the spirituality of service — will encourage the laity to become more deeply connected to their interior life so that God may be glorified through them.

The life of service unfolds in the midst of everyday life: work, school, meetings, soccer, bills, etc. How do we balance all of this with an interior life of pursuing God in prayer? Where do we find time for service? The answer is when service becomes prayer! *Discovering Christ the Servant* explores the intersection between the active life of service and the contemplative life of prayer allowing the lay person to see that by living their life in the daily pursuit of excellence, especially in loving cooperation with the grace of the sacraments, they will be inspired to give of themselves generously. When they learn more about the *why* of the Faith, lay people will naturally incorporate its tenets more deeply into the lived experience. This means growing daily in virtue and holiness through a life of prayer and sacrifice lived out in service to others while, at the same time, rediscovering the purpose of your life in the unfolding mystery of God's love.

The key themes and reflection questions that append each chapter provide a framework for either individual reflection or group discussion. This book can serve as a valuable resource for parish and diocesan staff retreats, lay formation programs, and diaconate continuing education classes. I can envision deacons and laity working through this book in small groups, with the pastor as the facilitator, as a way to better understand the vital role each plays in the life of the parish family and broader community.

Discovering Christ the Servant is a gift to the Church that every lay person should read, especially those who work with deacons. My prayer is that this labor of love, which is the fruit of Spirit-led contemplation, may help lay people and deacons appreciate the gift they are to each other so that we can more faithfully serve the people of God.

Deacon Harold Burke-Sivers, M.T.S.
Feast of Saints Simon and Jude,
October 28, 2021

Introduction
The Search for Intimacy

> *I fled Him, down the nights and down the days ...*
> *I fled Him, down the arches of the years;*
> *I fled Him, down the twisted corridors of my mind,*
> *   and hid beneath*
> *hollow laughter and in the midst of tears. ...*
> *   But with unhurrying chase,*
> *   and unperturbèd pace,*
> *   came on the following Feet ...*
> *For, though I knew the love of Him who followed,*
> *   my fear was that in having Him,*
> *   I must have naught beside.*
> **Francis Thompson, "The Hound of Heaven"**[1]

The title of this book, *Discovering Christ the Servant*, might strike some as a bit odd. I say "odd" because it's fair to assume that the selection of any text on spirituality implies that the reader has already discovered Christ and is now seeking a more intimate relationship with Him. While this is certainly true when the term *discovery* is used in a very narrow sense, it's never completely true. When it comes to persons, human or angelic, discovery isn't a static reality. It's not complete at any one point; rather, as long as it continues, it admits a dynamic quality. By this I mean that, when the relationship is healthy, we continue to discover and rediscover the other over time in a seemingly endless way.

If this seems somewhat vague, perhaps a simple analogy would be helpful. The beginning of any new relationship between a man and a woman, particularly one that will eventually blossom into marriage, begins with an initial discovery. The term "discovery" is used here to describe the revelation of something previously unknown, in this case, the meeting of the other person. In this initial meeting, the other is discovered, although in a very limited sense. Names are exchanged, small talk made, laughs shared, and perhaps even the mutual decision to meet again. To be sure, in such a first meeting, a discovery is made, but only in a very narrow sense. You come to know something about the other, but only something. What is left after this initial discovery is the strong desire to discover more. Should the relationship grow, this discovery deepens as more of the other is shared and as you share yourself. In this respect, discovery isn't a stagnant reality, but rather it takes on an ongoing property that continues through courtship, into marriage, and well beyond into the golden years.

To an infinitely greater extent, this dynamic characteristic is true of God as revealed in Christ Jesus. We discover Him and, because this discovery involves an ongoing relationship, we continue to discover Him in new and ever-deepening ways throughout our lives. What this book seeks to do is introduce the reader to a relatively unexplored aspect of God's Revelation, that of servanthood revealed by Jesus; hence the title *Discovering Christ the Servant*. However, before we get too far ahead of ourselves, it's important to apply this dynamic sense of discovery to our faith.

It's not uncommon, among those of us who are serious about our faith, to long for something more. This is true regardless of our spiritual maturity, or lack thereof. It typically starts as a yearning of the heart — often triggered during prayer or while at Mass — that gives rise to a sense of emptiness and an interior desire to move from where we are to where we need to be. This yearning is often persistent and unyielding and, while we struggle to fully grasp its import, we intuitively know that if we yield, our lives will gain greater meaning and satisfaction.

In the midst of living out our vocations, and even in the humdrum of everyday life, there's someone who beckons us, and that Someone is God. As poignantly expressed in the above passage by the English poet Francis Thompson, though we may elude Him for fear of what might be required of us, we nonetheless know, in the depths of our souls, that this longing isn't so much our search for Him, but rather His relentless pursuit of us. As odd as it may sound, it's He, despite our sinfulness (and even because of it), who desires us, longs for our company, hungers for our presence. It's His divine voice we hear in the stillness of our hearts, beckoning us to draw near. It's a voice that seeks to console us in the midst of our sorrows, to lift us when we are down, and to revel with us in times of joy. God wants to share in our lives so that we might more fully share in His (2 Pt 1:4). This is why, returning to Thompson's poem, He pursues us like a hound, unrelenting in His quest for a prize so dear to Him that He's willing to die for it. In order to allow ourselves to be found by God and, once found, to share in His life, progress in the spiritual life is essential. This is simply another way of talking about discovering and rediscovering God.

Talk of spiritual progress may seem somewhat out of place

and out of reach for the average Catholic and, in particular, for the very busy. This is true even among those who have more time on our hands. Most parish adult faith formation programs tend to focus on bible studies, catechetics, and prayer groups, while leaving the "deeper stuff," such as cultivating the interior life, for clergy and religious. Of course, even if we could find the time, could we find spiritual directors to guide us from where we are to a deeper, more intimate relationship with Jesus Christ? Unfortunately, trained spiritual directors are few and far between. Absent this, we could start reading the many spiritual classics, but where would we start, and who would help us integrate what we've learned into everyday life? As a result, many of us struggle with this inward longing and, in spite of God's unshakable call, end up dismissing spiritual growth as a passing thought amid a life already too demanding.

This struggle is by no means limited to the laity. It's common to everyone, saints and sinners alike. In celebrating the silver jubilee of my ordination a few years ago, I experienced a deep gratitude for the gift of Christ the Servant in my diaconate, in my marriage, in my fatherhood, and indeed in the whole of my life. This appreciation, interestingly enough, is made more profound by my recognition that I often struggle with the interior life. Sure, I pray the Divine Office, regularly receive spiritual direction, frequent the Sacrament of Reconciliation, partake in the Eucharist, and dutifully perform all the obligations associated with my vocation. Still, despite my calling to the diaconate, I'm not, at my core, a contemplative man, at least not in the sense that many of the saints and mystics were. It's not easy for me to suffer the presence of Christ at adoration or to meditate upon Him quietly for any significant period.

This struggle may seem rather strange and even scandalous to most of the laity, many of whom believe that clergy and religious have a natural inclination to prayer and the spiritual life. While many do, this inclination, which is part and parcel of their vocations, is often challenging because it requires a certain death-to-self, a willingness to let go and allow God to enter more deeply into their lives. This "letting go," this surrendering of self, isn't easy; and while with grace progress is made, it entails a lifelong process. As a result, the struggle with prayer as a means of cultivating a spiritual life is hardly exclusive to those called to a lay life. Rather, that same struggle impacts every person in every vocation, albeit in different ways.

As for me, strange as it may seem, this lack of a natural affinity for prayer, and the interior struggles associated with it, has brought me to an ever-increasing realization that what is difficult in the spiritual life is often necessary. This isn't to say that, over the years, I haven't made some slow progress, but rather that the progress I've made, with God's grace, has yet to bring me to the intimacy I so desire. In this struggle, I know I'm not alone.

A few years ago, acknowledging this challenge, and recognizing that others confront this same difficulty, I was moved to write a book specifically for deacons titled *Encountering Christ the Servant: A Spirituality of the Diaconate*. The work represents a spiritual journey for me. Over the past decade, I have developed a theology of the diaconate based on the thought of Pope St. John Paul II. In this pursuit, I was consoled by a Dominican approach to interiority that integrated the intellectual and spiritual aspects of life. Such an approach enabled me to experience theology as an encounter with the living God. One of St. Dominic de Guzmán's most significant contributions to the Catholic spiritual tradition is the belief that the theological endeavor, properly understood, isn't simply an aid to prayer, but an act of worship itself, an act that sanctifies.

Nowhere is this Dominican integration of the spiritual and intellectual life more beautifully illustrated than in an account of the thirteenth-century priest St. Thomas Aquinas. Saint Thomas was a towering figure in Catholic intellectual circles, having written volumes on a wide range of theological and philosophical issues. Yet at the same time, his intellect was only exceeded by his sanctity, as witnessed by the great hymns he wrote for the feast of Corpus Christi, hymns we still sing today. Toward the end of his life, Thomas was in the priory chapel, kneeling before the crucifix, absorbed in prayer, as was his usual practice. Unknown to him, Brother Dominic Caserta, a sacristan, was close by. Breaking the silence, a great voice boomed from the crucifix and, speaking to Thomas said, "You've written well of me Thomas. What will you have as your reward?" Saint Thomas answered, "Non nisi te Domine. Non nisi te." "Nothing but you, Lord. Nothing but you." Thomas understood well that the intellectual life is at the service of the spiritual life. His pursuit of truth, though noble in itself, was ultimately a pursuit of the Truth, Jesus Christ (Jn 14:6). In this respect, the only response Thomas could utter, the only response that made sense was "Non nisi te Domine." He knew, at the core of his being, that no reward is greater than intimate communion with God Himself.

Despite my struggles with the interior life, in the doing of theology, especially in plumbing the sources of Revelation, I have found myself wrapped in the Divine Presence. Theology is for me, as St. Anselm of Canterbury so succinctly put it, "faith seeking understanding." From this perspective, I can see that the teachings I study aren't cold, dispassionate doctrines, distinct and separate from my spiritual life, but, like Aquinas, truths that mediate the Truth. Theology, for me, isn't simply the search for something, but the discovery of Someone. It's about falling in love with God. In this sense, I have had an interior life that moves beyond a mere intellectual pursuit. Nonetheless, I had become slowly more aware that what has been lacking in me as a deacon is a deeper, more intimate communion with Christ the Servant. Sure, I know Him theologically in the Scriptures and

Tradition. I've experienced Him in worship through the sacraments. I've encountered Him pastorally in ministry and through being a husband and father. However, none of these, on their own, have brought the deep intimacy I so desire.

While writing my previous book, *Encountering Christ the Servant*, I gave some of the earlier drafts to a few of my lay friends to proofread. I wanted to ensure that the final manuscript sent to the publisher would be well polished and free of the errors typically associated with an initial submission. To my surprise and delight, they all indicated that much of what was written regarding the diaconate could be applied to the laity. This started me thinking about a second book — one that would use diaconal spirituality as a basis for a new lay spirituality, a spirituality of service. This made sense theologically.

Pondering this relationship between diaconal spirituality and a similar lay spirituality, I began to realize that what I had stumbled upon was no vague association, no tenuous link, but an intrinsic connection. The deacon, by virtue of his ordination, is called to bear witness to Christ the Servant; all of the faithful, by virtue of their Baptism, are called to serve — whether that be in formal ministry or in the living out of their often-frenzied lives. Put succinctly, all Christians are called to serve in imitation of Jesus. If this is true — and it is — then much of what was written in my prior book on diaconal spirituality could indeed be applied to a second work aimed at the laity. Such a book, and the spirituality it contains, could help others realize that a deeper, more intimate relationship with Jesus Christ is not out of reach, but well within the grasp of all who bear the name Christian. Such intimacy with Christ is not found by looking beyond the routines of diapers and feedings, late nights and early mornings, but it's precisely in and through the diapers and feedings, in and through the late nights and early mornings, that Christ the Servant is discovered, and discovered intimately.

Given the intrinsic relationship between diaconal spirituality and a lay spirituality of service, it's first necessary to introduce the reader to the diaconate. Because it's the deacon's mission to bear preeminent witness to Christ the Servant, any other approach to understanding Christian service would lack the full Christological dimension. Simply put, the diaconate provides the means by which to ground service in the person and mission of Jesus Christ. Nonetheless, some may argue that, since the deacon represents Christ as servant, and since the idea of religious service could be found apart from Christ, we needn't chart our way through the diaconate to provide a spirituality of lay service. This is certainly true in a limited and incomplete sense. We need only look to the patriarchs and prophets of the Old Testament to see service without a Christological dimension. However, while these examples certainly foreshadowed Christ the Servant, they did not reveal Him, and in not revealing Him, they lacked an essential fullness. Just as Jesus represents the fullness of the law and the prophets, He represents the fullness of service culminating in His passion, death, and resurrection.

Despite this, it could still be argued that many of the saints embraced an implicit servant spirituality without following the example of an active diaconate, though the diaconate has been with the Church since her inception. Again, this is true, but in a limited and incomplete sense. Christ the Servant was revealed most fully in Christ the Deacon (Mk 10:25; Mt: 20:28), and in this respect, the saints had a Christological grounding in sacred service and the spirituality that sourced it. However, just as Jesus' priesthood — while the perfect example of sacrifice — required an order of priests to perpetuate that sacrifice, so too Jesus' diaconate — while the perfect example of service — required an order of deacons to perpetuate that service. As we shall see further on, in my explanation of what I call the "Establishment Hypothesis," the use of orders to perpetuate Jesus' saving mission (expressed both in the priesthood and the diaconate) is not because His example is lacking in any way. Rather, it's because He wants us to share in His priesthood and His diaconate so as to share in His inner life by participating in His mission. Consequently, to bypass the diaconate in pursuit of a spirituality of service is to bypass something of Jesus Himself. Further, to do so is to bypass the quality that He brings to service, redemptive love. This is why an authentic and complete lay spirituality of service is not possible today without the diaconate and the indispensable role it plays in the Mystery of Salvation.[2]

Though much of what was written in *Encountering Christ the Servant* will be found in this book, the two books are far from identical. *Discovering Christ the Servant* proceeds with the lay person in mind and with the various vocational requirements that come from the lay state. Therefore, this book is meant to be a companion to the first book, such that deacons can share their spirituality with the laity, emboldening them to discover Christ the Servant anew and, in doing so, draw closer to Him. It will also have the secondary effect of catechizing the laity on the diaconate.[3]

This sharing of the diaconate with the laity is, in many respects, an essential part of the deacon's ministry. He's called, as we shall see in greater detail, to bear witness to Christ the Servant in a preeminent way. This book seeks to do this in two distinct but related ways. First, by providing a resource deeply rooted in Catholic Tradition and grounded in a spirituality of sacred service. Individuals reading *Discovering Christ the Servant* can come away with an interiority that can be integrated into their everyday lives, and thus grow closer to God. Second, by using this book as the main text in a parish share group, individuals can open themselves up to an even broader understanding of servant spirituality, especially in terms of its communal dimension. To facilitate both a personal internalization of servant spirituality and a communal sharing in a small group setting, I've included a section at the end of each chapter called "Meditations and Reflections." Though more will be said of this later, it includes a series of open-ended questions to be engaged through prayerful meditation. The questions are specifically designed to draw out what has been learned, the insights gained, and how these learnings and insights can be applied to everyday life. In this respect, servant spirituality — like many other spiritualities in the Catholic Tradition — can be adapted and applied such that, regardless of the uniqueness of our vocations, regardless of particular circumstances, and regardless of the busyness of our lives, Christ can be intimately discovered and encountered in the very fabric of our lives.

BEGINNING THE JOURNEY

Always remember this: life is a journey. It is a path, a journey to meet Jesus. At the end, and forever. ... It is for the Christian to continually encounter Jesus, to watch him, to let himself be watched over by Jesus, because Jesus watches us with love. ... To encounter Jesus also means allowing oneself to be gazed upon by him.
Pope Francis, Pastoral Visit to the Roman Parish of St. Cyril of Alexandria, December 1, 2013

All spiritual journeys begin with a call. It's an interior movement of the heart that beckons us to travel from where we are to where we need to be. The Church speaks of the Christian life in terms of a *call* or *vocation*, derived from the Latin term *vocatio*. Classically, vocations are divided into specific categories such as priestly, diaconal, married, consecrated, and lay. While helpful, such categorical distinctions, left unqualified, can hide more than they reveal. This is because we can fixate upon them such that we fail to see that they are means to a greater end. Pope St. John Paul II writes:

> God is love and in Himself He lives a mystery of personal loving communion. Creating the human race in His own image and continually keeping it in being, God inscribed in the humanity of man and woman the vocation, and thus the capacity and responsibility, of love and communion. Love is therefore the fundamental and innate vocation of every human being.[4]

Love of God and love of neighbor (Mk 12:30–31) constitute the universal vocation, that to which all human beings are called. The particular vocations (such as the priestly, diaconal, married, consecrated, and lay vocations) are ordered to this universal vocation. Put another way, particular vocations are the journey through which we experience the universal vocation — that is, intimate communion with God, which is a foretaste of heaven. To view our particular vocation as an end in itself is like looking at a pointing finger instead of looking at the direction in which the finger points. It fails to recognize that all of these vocations, regardless of what they are, are contextualized in their final end, love of God and love of neighbor. Understood this way, our vocation is not so much to something, but rather through something to Someone, Christ Jesus. This approach, rather than stressing the difference of each call, instead emphasizes what is common. In doing so, it reveals what is most essential and the end to which all human life is ordered.

Vocations, properly understood, must be lived from the inside out. This is because the call from God begins internally, within the deepest recesses of our being. It's here, with prudent discernment, that God makes Himself known to us; and it's also here that we make our response to Him. This interior response to this internal call is simply another way of speaking about spirituality. As we will see, the Catholic Tradition is replete with a great many complementary spiritualities, each providing a "road" of sorts upon which we journey from our own particular vocation to the universal vocation, the fulfillment of which is the heavenly vision. A person seriously seeking to live out his or her vocation must, by necessity, select a spirituality. To pursue a vocation without a spirituality is to begin a journey by meandering aimlessly, hoping to stumble upon the right road. Such an approach is fraught with frustration as it lacks a definite direction and established checkpoints in order to arrive at the intended end. Consequently, it's necessary to choose some way, some spirituality — and one that is marked by the successes of others, such as the saints of the Church, who traveled the same roads, finding that same end.

To accomplish this, and to make our spirituality truly our own, God leaves the choice open to us, as long as what we choose is consistent with our Catholic Faith. In this respect, we get to decide which of the many roads we'll take. Most do this rather implicitly, often cobbling together various spiritual traditions they've encountered throughout their lives. Others choose established spiritualities. In any case, the choice of a spirituality, the choice by which we respond to the divine call, marks the unique way in which we respond to God, and thereby live out our vocation in love and fidelity. It's important to note that the choice of a particular spirituality is not fixed such that, when one is chosen, it must be adhered to throughout the duration of our lives. We're free to "try on" different spiritualities to see if they fit, the true measure of which is the successful living out of our vocation. We are also free to mix and match over time, provided of course, what we choose is in harmony with our faith. This emphatically rules out such practices as New Age, Buddhist, Hindu, and universal spiritualities, to name a few.

In its most basic sense, spirituality in the Catholic Tradition means growth in holiness. It means personally appropriating and responding to the love of God as He's revealed through Christ and His Church. This requires — regardless of the kind of spirituality — cultivation of the interior life, which involves such practices as prayer, devotions, frequenting the sacraments, reading Scripture, meditation, and, where possible, spiritual direction. Servant spirituality is a specific kind of spirituality; it's a particular way of personally appropriating and responding to the love of God as He is made known through the Servant Mysteries. Broadly speaking, the Servant Mysteries are the revelation of Christ the Servant as He is manifested in the Scriptures, Tradition, Magisterium, and, in particular, the sacrament of the present moment — that is, in the ins and outs of our everyday lives. Simply put, a servant spirituality is one in which we can observe the Lord in serving others and, in that observation, encounter Him ourselves. In this respect, it's a lay form of diaconal spirituality where the object of our devotion is Christ the Servant, and the goal is intimate communion with Him through abandonment to His divine will. This abandonment, which is a lifelong process, enables us to bear witness to His spirit of service in our lives and, in particular, in the exercise of our vocations.

Because it's grounded in diaconal spirituality, servant spirituality may seem somewhat specialized, meant only for a select few. However, because it appeals to something universal and essential, it has application to all. This universal and essential characteristic will be taken up in greater detail in the next chapter. For now, it's sufficient to understand that Christian service doesn't just stand alongside other aspects of life; rather, it infuses everything. Indeed, as we shall see, it's not only a vital and necessary component to the saving mission of the Church, but it's also vital and necessary to our own salvation.

One of the defining features of servant spirituality is the

manner in which the interior life relates to the exterior life. Simply put, this feature concerns itself with how that which we believe on the inside impacts the choices we make on the outside. Here, the interior life forms and informs the exterior life, such that our growing intimacy with Christ finds its outward expression in the things we choose and in the lives we live. This dialectic between the inner and outer aspects of our lives will, like the essential characteristic of Christian service, be explored in greater detail as we progress through this work. Nonetheless, we can assert at this point that the interior life should permeate and penetrate the exterior life, enabling Christ the Servant to be revealed in the life of the believer. In this respect, servant spirituality avoids the dualism sometimes present in certain spiritualities that emphasize the interior life to the near exclusion of the exterior life.

Admittedly, the above description of servant spirituality and its impact on the exterior life could seem quite overwhelming, as it contains elements I have either not yet defined or not fully explained. A full treatment of the topic includes such terms as the cultivation of the interior life, the Servant Mysteries, the sacrament of the present moment, diaconal spirituality, intimate communion, and abandonment. For this initial deluge, I apologize to the reader! However, it's necessary at this early stage to familiarize you with these terms in their basic sense, to lay a foundation of sorts. Rest assured, as we proceed, we will unpack these terms, slowly and patiently piecing them together, resulting in a single concept captured in the phrase *servant spirituality*.

As introduced and presented in this book, servant spirituality is both old and new. It's old in that it draws heavily from the great Catholic spiritual traditions and is grounded in the ancient order of the diaconate. It's new because it arises out of a recent recovery of the theology and spirituality of the diaconate, along with its implications for all who are called to be servants of Christ. It's presented in this work because, just as it was out of divine providence that the Second Vatican Council restored the permanent diaconate for our day and age, so too it's believed that the spirituality of the same diaconate is, by divine providence, likewise meant for our day and age. In this respect, if the unique contribution of the diaconate is to bear preeminent witness to Christ the Servant to the whole Church, so too its spirituality is meant to enable laity and clergy alike to discover, from the inside out, that same Christ who came not to be served, but to serve.

In all of this, great emphasis is placed on situating our consideration of servant spirituality within the broader Catholic spiritual and mystical traditions, providing a sense of continuity with those very same traditions. To that end, quotes of saints and mystics are sprinkled throughout, adding a depth and texture to what is discussed. In this respect, while servant spirituality as expressed in this book is relatively new, the tradition from which it emerges is ancient and rich. This, along with recent theological developments, provides the necessary framework on which to build an authentically Catholic servant spirituality.

Given the above approach, and in order to plumb the depths of this spirituality, it will be necessary to begin by laying the theological groundwork. It's here where some, having a limited sense of the discipline of theology, might begin to worry. They need not. Without a theological basis, a spirituality of service — and indeed, any Christian spirituality — would be significantly diminished because it wouldn't be rooted in the sources of Revelation revealing the love of God. Such a lack would result in a generic, almost New Age, kind of spirituality, absent any substantial connection to Tradition. Consequently, it will be necessary, at least in the following chapter, to ground servant spirituality in its theological context. Here, I will make a conscious effort to "walk" the reader slowly through this approach, so that the richness of the theological contribution is appreciated for what it is, a deeper reflection on the Revelation of God Himself.

This book is written with the laity in mind as its primary reader, though the clergy and religious can certainly benefit from it. It assumes, as a basis for a servant spirituality, one who is a practicing Catholic, moderately catechized, with a regular prayer life, and one who frequents the sacraments, especially Reconciliation and Eucharist. While these elements are not absolutely necessary to draw insights from this book, their presence, as illustrated in the Parable of the Sower (Mt 13:1–23), will bear a richer harvest. Nonetheless, for those who find themselves lacking in one or more of these areas, be at peace. Instead, press on with the book and pursue these elements as part and parcel of building a solid foundation for the interior life. In this respect, consistent practice of the Faith, ongoing catechesis, regular prayer, and the reception of the sacraments are all elements that can be adopted and further developed in the ongoing and never-ending desire to cultivate the interior life. While this book will address these elements within the context of a lay spirituality of service, it will not provide a general introduction for the unfamiliar. In this regard, the reader should seek other basic sources through their parish and trusted Catholic publications.[5] Still, the context given in this work, combined with grace, will provide enough for the unfamiliar to become more familiar and, in doing so, draw closer to Christ the Servant.

In writing this book and presenting my thoughts, I don't wish to imply that I'm some sort of spiritual master, or even an authority in mystical and spiritual theology. I come as simply one poor beggar showing other poor beggars where the food is. In fact, this work merely represents my own ponderings as they've been shaped by my own particular theological and spiritual formation within the Catholic Tradition. I'm convinced that what I've stumbled upon isn't meant for me and me alone, but for any and all who might benefit from it. In this I humbly lay at your feet, my dear readers, whatever worth you find in this book, so that, together and in union with Him, we may bear witness to Christ the Servant, fulfilling our vocations and contributing to the mission of the Church.

One final note before beginning. Do not let the brevity of this book fool you. It's packed with insights, insights that need to be carefully unpacked in the heart of the reader. If this book is read in a cursory way, it will reveal little and later sit on the shelf only to collect dust. Instead, I invite the reader to read this text in a deeply prayerful and contemplative state. Take it in small bits, asking Our Lord to reveal in your heart what you need to know and how that revelation is to impact the whole of your life. Look for yourself between the pages, and discover in your reflection who you are, and who you're called to be. Patiently waiting for you within these very same pages is none other than Christ the Servant. Go and meet Him with great joy and anticipation.

INTERNALIZING A SERVANT SPIRITUALITY

Often when we're introduced to new ideas and concepts, especially those of a spiritual nature, a single pass through isn't enough. This means that what we discover in the initial encounter represents merely a small part of an infinitely larger Truth — that is, God Himself. Because this smaller truth is organically related to greater truths and ultimately to the Truth Himself, it has the potential to unfold over time under the influence of the Holy Spirit. In this respect, what we have encountered so far, and what we will encounter throughout this book, is seminal in nature. Carrying the metaphor further, this means that, by tilling and fertilizing the soil, the seed has the very real potential to germinate and eventually bear fruit. In a similar way, through prayerful reflection and meditation, the truths we encountered in each chapter have the potential to reveal yet greater truths. Consequently, if the reader desires more than just a cursory understanding of what he or she has read, and desires authentic spiritual growth, then a means is necessary to internalize these truths such that, from them, the interior life is cultivated. This cultivation requires a special kind of communication with God.

It's been said that many pray to God, yet few speak with Him. This is to say that quite often praying amounts to a one-way conversation. Whether it's praise or adoration, thanksgiving or contrition, intercession or petition, our prayers can be one-sided. Part of this may be because we were never taught to pray in a way that included listening, and another part may be because we're afraid of what we might hear should we listen. Though any form of prayer, when done with an open heart, is pleasing to God, God wants to communicate with us. He wants to share something of Himself with us in a deeply personal way. Because of this, speaking with God in prayer — which involves both talking and listening — is superior to simply praying to Him. In speaking with God, we're attentive to what He has to say to us; we are setting up an ongoing dialogue and strengthening our relationship with Him. Beyond this, as we listen, our own contribution to the conversation changes for the better, having been shaped by what we've heard.

The practice of internalizing a servant spirituality will involve the reader meditating and reflecting upon the material in an ongoing manner. In order to facilitate a second, more thorough, pass through without being redundant, a final section is included. Each chapter ends with "Meditations and Reflections," which include "Key Themes" and "Questions for Reflection." As mentioned earlier, this section includes a series of two integrated spiritual exercises: one focusing on prayerful meditation and the other on interior reflection. Together, these will allow for a deeper, more profound dive into the material, with the aim of internalizing it.

To those unfamiliar with meditation as a form of prayer, this may seem somewhat daunting. While there is some truth to this, it's equally true that, when aided by grace, meditation can be a great source of spiritual insight, even for those unacquainted with the practice. According to the *Catechism of the Catholic Church*, "Meditation is above all a quest. The mind seeks to understand the why and how of the Christian life, in order to adhere and respond to what the Lord is asking."[6] In simple but profound language, the *Catechism* continues by saying:

> To meditate on what we read helps us to make it our own by confronting it with ourselves. Here, another book is opened: the book of life. We pass from thoughts to reality. To the extent that we are humble and faithful, we discover in meditation the movements that stir the heart and we are able to discern them. (2706)

Applied to our pursuit, the meditations found at the end of each chapter provide a means to discover the *why* and *how* of servant spirituality as it relates to intimate communion with Christ the Servant. This ever-deepening intimacy becomes the very source of a life lived in grace. Affirming this truth, St. Ignatius of Loyola, commenting on the importance of meditation, writes, "Meditation consists in calling to mind some ... truth and reflecting on or discussing this truth according to each one's capacity, so as to move the will and produce in us amendment."[7] In order to tie the meditations directly into what was previously read, they are grounded in key themes extracted from the chapter. These themes are designed to reengage the reader with the material, enriching the earlier conversation by advancing it. It's precisely through this conversation — through this back-and-forth, immersed in prayer — that the reader will appreciate, more fully, the "voice" of God.

As an integrated second step in this process, following the meditations there are a series of six reflection questions. Each is specifically designed to offer a more in-depth, yet accessible, grasp of what was "heard" in the meditations. While this method will be discussed in greater detail at the end of each chapter, the combination of meditations and reflections have the real potential to stimulate spiritual growth. All of this will require some work on the part of the reader, but rest assured, it's a work aided by grace which, in the end, finds its consolation in Christ the Servant. As Archbishop Ven. Fulton J. Sheen was quick to point out, "Whenever man attempts to do what he knows to be the Master's will, a power will be given him equal to the duty."[8]

Whether in reading, meditating, or reflecting, take care to write down your insights in a prayer journal or spiritual notebook. Where a prayer journal resembles a diary, having almost daily entries on the interior life, the entries in a spiritual notebook are occasioned by the thoughts and insights gleaned in prayer and living the Christian life. Simply put, while journals recount the events of the day from a spiritual perspective (and, in this respect, are more obliging), spiritual notebooks are typically prompted by events (and, because these events may be less frequent, they are less obliging). This distinction is not universal, but it does help those who use neither a journal nor a spiritual notebook. At first, they may be overwhelmed at the thought of daily entries and thus, if and when insights don't come on a regular basis, feel discouraged. Consequently, it's good to start with a notebook and, should insights begin to come on a regular basis, the notebook will automatically turn into a journal. In any case, the recording of thoughts and insights is invaluable to the spiritual life. As St. Francis Xavier observed:

> When you meditate on all these things, I earnestly advise you to write down, as a help to your memory, those heavenly lights which our merciful God so often gives to the soul which draws near to Him, and with which He

will also enlighten yours when you strive to know His will in meditation, for they are more deeply impressed on the mind by the very act and occupation of writing them down. And should it happen, as it usually does, that in course of time these things are either less vividly remembered or entirely forgotten, they will come with fresh life to the mind by reading them over.[9]

MEDITATIONS AND REFLECTIONS

As discussed above, this final section is designed to allow a deeper, more personal absorption of the material just covered. It consists of a set of two interrelated spiritual exercises whose sole purpose is to reengage the key themes from the previous readings so as to internalize the truths they contain. This approach is based on the fundamental conviction that by prayerfully reflecting and meditating on these truths, God wants to speak to you in a way that will draw you into a deeper, more intimate communion with Christ the Servant. Each exercise should begin with at least a minute or two of relaxed silence, disposing your heart to the encounter. This should be followed by either a short extemporaneous prayer or, if you choose, the following:

Heavenly Father, I open my heart up to You so that, through the power of Your most Holy Spirit, I may encounter your Son, Christ the Servant, in a deeply personal and transformative way. Forgive my sins and free me from the attachments of this world so that I am better attentive to Your presence and, in this attentiveness, hear what You want me to hear. Give me the grace to abandon myself to You in this moment for, in the depths of my soul, I want nothing more than You. Speak, Lord, Your servant listens. Mary, Mother of Christ the Servant, pray for me. Amen.

KEY THEMES

The following represent some key themes found in this chapter. As you reflect on them, consider what Christ the Servant is revealing about Himself and, more importantly, what He's revealing about you. In this, you're asking two distinct but related questions: Lord, what are You saying *in general*; and, flowing from this, what are You saying specifically *to me*? Ponder how that which is said may impact your relationship with Him — and how it may influence your relationships with others, particularly in the choices you make. Remember, as you meditate upon these things, write down your thoughts in your journal or spiritual notebook. This could consist of a single word, a sentence, a paragraph, or even more. The purpose here is to capture the most important elements of your meditation, even if they are not whole or complete.

Bear in mind that what is offered in these exercises is by way of a pious recommendation. You are free to fully engage or completely omit them as you see fit. Should you decide to move forward, you may take on one, some, or even all of the themes as the Spirit prompts you. This exercise and its effectiveness rely on grace and your openness to that grace. With all of this in mind, the key themes of this introduction are as follows:

- Longing for something more
- Importance of growth in the spiritual life
- Theology as "faith seeking understanding"
- Servant spirituality
- Vocation as an interior call
- Speaking with God

REFLECTION QUESTIONS

Now that you have meditated upon these themes and captured what Christ the Servant may be saying to you, you can explore them further in the following six reflection questions. It's recommended that this be done in a separate sitting, giving you a chance to digest the fruit of your initial meditation. Should you choose to follow this recommendation, begin again with silence and prayer, as described above. As with the themes, write down your insights and thoughts in your journal or spiritual notebook.

- Identify two or three things you learned from this chapter that you didn't know before.
- Identify two or three key insights you gained through this chapter that speak to your spiritual life, family, God, or the Church.
- Identify two or three ways to apply your learning and insights from this chapter to your life as a Catholic.
- Based on what you have learned so far, what part does deepening your *relationship to Christ the Servant* play in developing a servant spirituality?
- Based on what you have learned so far, what part does deepening your *identity in Christ the Servant* play in developing a servant spirituality?
- Based on what you have learned so far, what part does deepening your *mission with Christ the Servant* play in developing a servant spirituality?

Chapter One
A Spirituality Rooted in the Diaconate

To fulfill his mission, the deacon therefore needs a deep interior life, sustained by the exercises of piety recommended by the Church. Carrying out ministerial and apostolic activities, fulfilling possible family and social responsibilities and, lastly, practicing an intense personal life of prayer required of the deacon, whether celibate or married, that unity of life which can only be attained, as Vatican Council II taught, through deep union with Christ.
Pope St. John Paul II, Address to the Plenary Assembly of the Congregation for the Clergy, October 6, 1993

As noted earlier, servant spirituality is rooted in diaconal spirituality. The intrinsic connection between the two arises out of a universal call to follow Jesus, who "did not come to be served but to serve" (Mk 10:45). What is true of Jesus is also true of His Mystical Body, the Church. All, by virtue of Baptism, are called to love one another by serving one another (Jn 13:12–15). This means that the Church is, at her very core, a servant Church, and it's precisely through this service that she carries out her saving mission. Both diaconal spirituality and servant spirituality are, in many respects, quite similar, with the difference being their vocational applications. Where servant spirituality is applied to the many vocations of the laity, diaconal spirituality is applied to the vocation of the diaconate. The commonality they share is sacred service. The uniqueness they possess is how that service is carried out, such that the two admit to a kind of complementarity, each bringing to the mission of the Church something the other does not; each revealing Christ the Servant in a way the other cannot.

To better appreciate the essential relationship between diaconal and servant spirituality, an analogy to the priesthood might be helpful. According to the *Catechism*:

> The ministerial or hierarchical priesthood of bishops and priests, and the common priesthood of all the faithful participate, "each in its own proper way, in the one priesthood of Christ." While being "ordered one to another," they differ essentially. In what sense? While the common priesthood of the faithful is exercised by the unfolding of baptismal grace — a life of faith, hope, and charity, a life according to the Spirit — the ministerial priesthood is at the service of the common priesthood. It is directed at the unfolding of the baptismal grace of all Christians. The ministerial priesthood is a *means*

by which Christ unceasingly builds up and leads his Church. (1547)

What is true of the priesthood and the laity should, in many respects, be likewise true of the diaconate and the laity. Could not the above passage be reconfigured to reflect the relationship between the diaconate and the laity, between diaconal spirituality and a lay spirituality of service? If it could, then it might read:

> The ministerial or hierarchical diaconate, and the common diaconate of all the faithful participate, each in its own proper way, in the one diaconate of Christ. While being ordered one to another, they differ essentially. In what sense? While the common diaconate of the faithful is exercised by the unfolding of baptismal grace — a life of faith, hope, and charity, a life according to the Spirit — the ministerial diaconate is at the service of the common diaconate. It is directed at the unfolding of the baptismal grace of all Christians. The ministerial diaconate is a means by which Christ unceasingly builds up and serves his Church.

In the above analogy, the laity, by virtue of Baptism, are configured to Christ, who is both deacon and priest. Jesus Himself reveals this complementary identity when He says, "Just so, the Son of Man did not come to be served but to serve [diaconate] and to give his life as a ransom [priesthood] for many" (Mt 20:28). Both the diaconate and priesthood find their nexus in the one Christ to whom all of the faithful are united in Baptism. Therefore it follows that, just as there is an intrinsic connection between the diaconate and laity, there is similarly an intrinsic connection between diaconal spirituality and servant spirituality. Both are absolute preconditions for a ministry of service. Both are necessary if the Church is to effectively fulfill her mission.

For many — clergy and laity alike — this vocational connection may seem rather unusual and even odd. This seeming oddity, I suspect, arises out of a fundamental misunderstanding of the diaconate. Unfortunately, many, if not most, see the deacon as a kind of glorified altar boy or junior priest. The order is often viewed as a kind of retirement ministry, meant to help out overworked priests. In large measure, this misunderstanding arose out of an undeveloped theology of the diaconate, in which the life and the ministry of the deacon has been virtually unknown to much of the Church. I say this as very little is taught about the diaconate in major seminaries, leaving many priests and bishops without a clear understanding of the order.[1] Sadly, the same is true of many diaconal formation programs. This lack of clarity has negatively impacted the way the Church understands Christ the Servant and the way in which all are called to serve, each according to his or her own vocation. Consequently, unless the diaconate is better known, unless its theological "place" is recovered from the Scriptures and Tradition, its spirituality will be impoverished, and with it the ability to serve as Christ served. This ability, which is a response to grace, enables us to incarnate Jesus in our actions, enabling us to effectively fulfill our role in the Mystery of Salvation. Thus, as we've already seen, before we can adequately lay out a servant spirituality for the laity, it will be necessary to address diaconal spirituality, as both are intrinsically related. This is because servant spirituality finds its roots in the origins of the diaconate. In this respect, while the primary purpose of this book is to introduce a servant spirituality to the laity, its secondary but equally important purpose is to unfold the diaconate to that same laity. The two purposes, as we shall see, are indispensable to one another.

TOWARD A CLEARER UNDERSTANDING OF SERVICE

It's not necessary, for our objectives, to go into great detail concerning the nature of the diaconate. We need only cover two key elements that will aid in our understanding of servant spirituality. These include: First, a proper understanding of the term *service*; and, second, the origins of Holy Orders as it relates to the whole Church. The Greek word *diákonos*, commonly rendered as *servant* or *minister*, was probably derived from the obsolete verb *diōkō*, meaning "to run errands." Though rare in Classical Greek, and uncommon in the Greek Old Testament, the *diakon* word group appears in some form over a hundred times in the New Testament. In his contribution to the *Theological Dictionary of the New Testament*, the German scholar Hermann W. Beyer held that the verb *diakoneō* means simply "to serve" or "to provide and care for." He was highly influenced by other Protestant scholars who, in turn, were influenced by the Lutheran Deaconess Movement of the late nineteenth century. By this time, the standard German term *diakonie*, a transliteration of *diakonia*, had come to designate social work. It was from this secular association that Beyer saw a strong parallel to Christian service. This understanding was picked up and circulated by many of the lesser-known lexicons and commentaries of the time. Since Catholic scholars, after the restoration of the diaconate by the Second Vatican Council, used these Protestant interpretations, having established none of their own, and since these sources were far more concerned with ministry than with scriptural or patristic usage, the Catholic understanding followed the Protestant concept of *diákonos* as one who serves the poor and needy.

This rather widespread notion of service was challenged in 1990 by the Australian linguist John N. Collins. In his groundbreaking book *Diakonia: Re-Interpreting the Ancient Sources*,

Collins focuses on the nature and function of Christian ministry.[2] He conducts an exhaustive study of the term *diakonia* using both Christian and non-Christian sources from about 200 BC to AD 200. Collins concludes that, in all of these sources, the term means an *envoy, emissary,* or *messenger* and has little to do with care for the poor and needy as such. Instead, he maintains that Jesus' *diakonia* is done out of compassion and love for others *as an envoy of the Father*.[3]

Collins brilliantly puts the emphasis of Christian service back where it belongs, shifting the object of *diakonia* (ministerial service) away from the thing being done to a concrete expression of divine love. This is what it really means to be a minister of service: not simply a doer of good things, but an envoy of God's love in the service of which good things are done. The deacon's service isn't first and foremost to the people, but to God, and only in God, and with His grace, can he truly serve the people.

What is true of the deacon is equally true of the laity, albeit configured to their own particular vocation. Understood this way, the implication of Collins's contribution moves Christian service away from a purely functional work to a deeply relational encounter. Here, the deacon is called to stand in-between God and the people as a divine ambassador and proclaim the Gospel, which is precisely what he does in the liturgy. Collins's breakthrough undercuts much of the theological discussion on the diaconate that has taken place since its restoration by the Fathers of the Second Vatican Council. This development has implications not merely for the diaconate but, insofar as all of the baptized are called to serve, on all who bear the name Christian.

By re-envisioning *diakonia* and re-anchoring it in the language of the Early Church as an envoy or messenger of divine love, Collins implicitly presupposes an intimate relationship of trust and responsibility between the servant and God. This is why the cultivation of the interior life is essential to living out our "diaconate," whether it's as a deacon or laity, as it provides the "interior place" to know and love the One who sends us. It's precisely this love that becomes the primary motivation for Christian service, be it as a deacon or layperson. It sources their strength in the One who sends them, thereby enriching their lives and ministry with a distinctively divine quality. Without this essential quality, the laity become mere functionaries, losing the relational characteristic proper to an envoy of Christ.

Before exploring the second key element in our understanding of servant spirituality, it's crucial to grasp the universal importance of the diaconate as it relates to the entire Church. The ancient diaconate was originally instituted, and then restored in our time, not simply to stand alongside priestly, religious, and lay ministry, but instead to infuse and empower each of the other vocations with a renewed sense of service. Indeed, the Greek word *diakonia*, which is translated in English as *service*, can also be translated into the Latin word *ministerium* which, in turn, in English is *ministry*. Thus, when we refer to episcopal ministry, priestly ministry, religious ministry, or lay ministry, the term *ministry* or *diakonia* is essential to all. In this respect, the diaconate was instituted and restored in our times, and for our times, to remind the Church of Christ the Servant. It instills in the hearts of all a sense that the Gospel is to be lived in imitation of Jesus. In this sense, service isn't something we do, but rather it's someone we give; namely, our very selves. It's an act of human love rooted in a divine love already outpoured. This is a radical, but nonetheless thoroughly consistent, rethinking of Christian service that takes up the Tradition and builds upon it in ways that are both old and new.

THE ORIGINS OF HOLY ORDERS

> *Ephrem, honored by Christian tradition with the title "Harp of the Holy Spirit," remained a deacon of the Church throughout his life. It was a crucial and emblematic decision: he was a deacon, a servant, in his liturgical ministry, and more radically, in his love for Christ, whose praises he sang in an unparalleled way, and also in his love for his brethren, whom he introduced with rare skill to the knowledge of divine Revelation.*
> **Pope Benedict XVI, General Audience, November 28, 2007**

Earlier, I observed that many in the Church today have a very limited understanding of the diaconate. This wasn't always the case, beginning with the very first martyr:

> When they heard this, they were infuriated, and they ground their teeth at him. But he, filled with the holy Spirit, looked up intently to heaven and saw the glory of God and Jesus standing at the right hand of God, and he said, "Behold, I see the heavens opened and the Son of Man standing at the right hand of God." But they cried out in a loud voice, covered their ears, and rushed upon him together. They threw him out of the city, and began to stone him. The witnesses laid down their cloaks at the feet of a young man named Saul. As they were stoning Stephen, he called out, "Lord Jesus, receive my spirit." Then he fell to his knees and cried out in a loud voice, "Lord, do not hold this sin against them"; and when he said this, he fell asleep. (Acts 7:54–60)

A Spirituality Rooted in the Diaconate 45

It's worth noting that the first believer to follow Christ in death for proclaiming the Gospel wasn't an apostle, bishop, or even presbyter (priest), but instead a deacon, Saint Stephen. In his first letter to Timothy, Saint Paul describes the qualities of a good deacon, revealing the place of the diaconate in the heart and imagination of the early Church.[4] After Pentecost, as the Church spread, she was met with periods of persecution followed by periods of toleration. That would change with the Edict of Milan in AD 313, coauthored by the Emperors Constantine in the West and Licinius in the East. In that imperial decree, Rome agreed to treat Christians benevolently within the Empire. After this, the Church grew rapidly and, with her, the diaconate.

Up until the eighth century, deacons enjoyed a close, filial relationship with their bishops. They were to be his ears, eyes, mouth, and heart. In many places, deacons were appointed administrators of large pastoral regions, with presbyters assigned to smaller areas known as *tituli* (parishes). Deacons functioned liturgically, organized charitable work, and brought a portion of the bishop's Eucharist (*fermentum*) to the presbyterate. In Rome they enjoyed unprecedented influence, as demonstrated in their ascension to the papacy. Of the thirty-seven men elected pope between AD 432 and 684, only three are known to have been ordained to the priesthood before their election to the Chair of Peter. All the rest were chosen directly from the diaconate. A shift in the understanding of the priesthood, the abuse of their office by some deacons, and the adoption of the Roman practice of moving from a lower office to a higher office (*cursus honororum*), led to the diaconate moving from a permanent order to a transitional one. As a result, by the eighth century, with some rare exceptions (St. Francis of Assisi being one of them), the diaconate became a steppingstone to the priesthood. Consequently, the theological development of Holy Orders through subsequent centuries focused almost exclusively on the priesthood.

By the time the diaconate was restored to a permanent order by the Fathers of the Second Vatican Council, there was virtually no theology of the diaconate. This is to say, because of its long absence in the Latin Church, there was almost no sense of what the diaconate is or what its relationship to other aspects of the Faith are. Without a developed theology in place, there was little understanding of the order, except that which had been done by Protestant scholars a century earlier. This is the reason why, as noted earlier, the Church today has had a very limited grasp of the diaconate. If servant spirituality is based on diaconal spirituality, and if diaconal spirituality is rooted in the theology of the diaconate, then it would be first necessary to develop (or rediscover from ancient sources) a theology of the diaconate. This theology, in turn, would make possible a diaconal spirituality which, as a result, would give rise to a servant spirituality.

Following this logical progression, while my first book — *In the Person of Christ the Servant* — focused on a theology of the diaconate, and the second — *Encountering Christ the Servant* — on diaconal spirituality, this third book takes up servant spirituality for the laity.[5] Like three building blocks stacked one on top of the other, this approach provides the basis for a servant spirituality by demonstrating its connection to Christ the Servant within the Mystery of Salvation. To better appreciate what I mean here, we will briefly consider the origins of Holy Orders.

This consideration may seem somewhat out of place as Holy Orders has to do with the clergy, whereas servant spirituality has to do with the laity. It could be asked, "Aren't these vocations distinct and separate?" In some ways they are, and in some ways they're not. To be sure, they're separate vocations, but they're also related, and because they're related they share an organic connection. So, for example, just as my heart and my brain are clearly distinct, they're intrinsically related. One is very much dependent on the other for its existence, and both find their nexus in my one body. In much the same way, just as the clergy and the laity are clearly distinct, they too are intrinsically related. One is very much dependent on the other for its existence, and both find their nexus in the one Body — that is, the Church. Therefore, a consideration of Holy Orders, as it relates to the Mystery of Salvation, will prove decisive in demonstrating the unique role of the laity in the mission of the Church. More specifically, it will show how that role is revealed by Christ in and through the diaconate as a gift to the laity; a gift that also includes servant spirituality.

One of the challenges in our consideration of the origins of Holy Orders is that, while the Church has treated this topic within her Tradition, the lack of a theology of the diaconate meant that it was incomplete. She most certainly has a strong understanding of the beginnings of the priesthood and a somewhat less developed but still substantial sense of the episcopacy. Nonetheless, theological explanations for the diaconate, as we've already observed, have been largely deficient. However, some recent strides in diaconal theology now make it possible to offer a more comprehensive understanding of the origins of Holy Orders. This new approach reveals not only the complementary relationship among bishops, priests, and deacons, but the complementary relationship between the clergy and laity in God's plan of salvation.

While writing my first book, I quite providentially stumbled upon a way in which the Church might better describe the unity of Holy Orders. Using the personalist thought of Pope St. John Paul II, I discovered the philosophical language that would provide the ability to grasp more clearly the meaning of Christian service as it relates to diaconal ministry and to all who follow Christ. For those unfamiliar with theological development, talk of philosophical language may seem somewhat strange and out-of-place. However, in the Catholic Tradition, philosophy is considered the handmaid of theology (*ancilla theologiae*), with greats such as St. Augustine of Hippo relying on the thought of Neoplatonists, and St. Thomas Aquinas employing the work of Aristotle.

Non-Christian ways of speaking are often borrowed, modified, and applied anew to tease out a truth already present. In much the same way a nonbeliever can become a believer through Baptism, philosophical language can be "baptized," so-to-speak, sanctifying its use. Thus, for example, Saint Thomas was able to describe the Real Presence of Christ in the Eucharist more clearly by using Aristotle's metaphysics (CCC 1413). Similarly, Pope St. John Paul II used personalist philosophy in a great many of his teachings.[6] Taking his work, I applied it to the diaconate, revealing new insights, insights previously hidden and now made known — the most fascinating of which is service as a "gift-of-self." Here, diaconal ministry, or any Christian service for that matter, is not so much something we do, but rather someone we give, our very selves.

This insight is as simple as it is profound, moving the language of service away from a depersonalized function to an interpersonal reality. In serving others, it's not so much that I do something extrinsic and apart from me, but rather that I, in the very doing of that something, give an intrinsic part of myself. I pour myself out to the very person I serve as a free gift, just as Christ did on the cross, in which I am following His example. This imbues Christian service with a particular quality, such that it's not so much what I do, but how I do what I do. St. Francis Xavier understood this when he said, "It is not the actual physical exertion that counts toward a man's progress, nor the nature of the task, but the spirit of Faith with which it is undertaken." This spirit of Faith is not simply the Faith of the Church, but rather, the faith of the Church as that faith infuses me, transforms me, and motivates me to love others. It's precisely this faith, through grace, that I am capacitated to gift myself to another.

Of course, not all gifts are equal. We don't gift ourselves to our parishioners or friends the same way we might gift ourselves to our children and spouses. The nature of the relationship determines the kind of gift, and the degree to which it's given. Where marriage, by nature of the sacramental love it possesses, requires the highest kind and degree of love for another human being, the gift-of-self to God is in a completely different category. Unlike our spouses, God, the First Giver, has given us everything. He is our Creator, Redeemer, and Sanctifier. As a result, our response-gift to Him must be our all, total and complete. Indeed, because of a fallen yet redeemed human nature, this requires grace and a lifetime of effort on our part. Thus, we can speak of our response-gift as a dynamic that, over time, has the potential to grow or diminish depending on our willingness to give.

As we shall see later in our treatment of abandonment, these gifts we make of ourselves, these acts of love expressed in service, don't represent a zero-sum gain. This is to say that the gift I make to one doesn't, by that fact, decrease the gift to another. In fact, quite the opposite is true. In gifting myself selflessly to another, my capacity to give myself to others increases. I become, in that act, a more giving person, imbuing my service with the quality of divine love, thereby revealing Christ the Servant. This requires a certain intentionality in the giving, a certain interior conscious act of the will, to offer myself without expecting anything in return. To appreciate what I mean here, consider the opposite. As you've no doubt experienced, it's quite possible to pray without actually praying, go to Mass without actually going to Mass, and even love without actually loving. This is because it's not sufficient simply to go through the actions on the outside without going through a corresponding set of actions on the inside (in philosophy, these inner actions are called *intentionality*). An approach that consists only of "going through the motions" empties the act of its authentic meaning because, regardless of the nature of the relationship, lack of intentionality results in only giving part of what is required. In this respect, such action is lacking in both justice and charity to the one being served, rendering the act void of its natural end.

This gift-of-self, which is simply another way of speaking about love, intrigued me, especially as it's played out in the Paschal Mystery. As a result, by applying Pope St. John Paul's personalist thought, I not only had the language needed to better describe diaconal service, but, quite providentially, I also had the language to better describe the unity of Holy Orders, both of which reveal and exemplify an authentic servant spirituality. It was while reflecting on this insight that I discovered what I would come to call the "Establishment Hypothesis." This will be discussed in greater detail as we proceed, but for now it's enough to say the Establishment Hypothesis situates Holy Orders and Christian service within the context of a human love sourced in divine love. This gives Christian service its definitive characteristic.[7] In order to better appreciate what I mean, I will ask your patience as I walk you through the theology that underlies Christian service. Regardless of your familiarity with the discipline of theology, the insights arising from our study will be well worth the effort. I, for my part, will break it down into specific and well-defined steps, keeping you in mind as I do so.

The Establishment Hypothesis is grounded in three fundamental principles. The first and most important of these is the centrality of the Paschal Mystery. Indeed, as described in the *Compendium of the Catechism of the Catholic Church*, "The Paschal Mystery of Jesus, which comprises his passion, death, resurrection, and glorification, stands at the center of the Christian Faith because God's saving plan was accomplished once for all by the redemptive death of his Son Jesus Christ."[8] This, of course, is the core belief of all Christians and an essential doctrine of the Catholic Church. Simply put, the Paschal Mystery is what makes Christian doctrine authentically Christian. Second, this redemption is offered by God, through His Church, by way of Holy Orders. Hence, according to the *Catechism*, "Holy Orders is the sacrament through which the mission entrusted by Christ to his apostles continues to be exercised in the Church until the end of time: thus it is the sacrament of apostolic ministry" (1536). By the will of God, without Holy Orders — without bishops, priests, and deacons — Christ's saving mission would have ceased at His ascension. As a result, it's inconceivable for a Catholic to think of salvation outside the saving power of Christ's word and sacraments, which are dispensed to the faithful, historically and today, by those in Holy Orders.

Third, just as the Paschal Mystery is nothing less than a divine gift-of-self, an outpouring of divine love, so too it's perpetuated through a similar gift-of-self in the three degrees of Holy Orders. This understanding of love, as noted earlier, was, for me, radical and revolutionary. To be sure, I understood love within the Catholic Tradition as willing the good of the other for the sake of the other; however, this new understanding of love as a gift-of-self moves love from a desire of the will to concrete acts, which was implied in the Tradition, but not fleshed out in the same way.[9] This was the key contribution of Pope St. John Paul II to my thinking and, theologically, it made complete sense — raising the Tradition to a whole new level. Christ's entire life from His Incarnation through His passion, death, resurrection, ascension, and future coming is nothing less than a gift-of-self. This gift-of-self, unlike all others, is absolutely unique and utterly unrepeatable because it's an exercise of divine love, which is unconditional and knows no limits.

Nowhere is this more vividly expressed than in the crucifixion, where our Lord gifts Himself to all of humanity for all time. Jesus doesn't simply will our good in some sentimental or abstract way. Instead, He ensures that good by sacrificially offering Himself to us in a concrete act of love that boggles the imagination. As beautifully expressed in the *Catechism*, "When the hour had come for him to fulfill the Father's plan of love, Jesus allows a glimpse of the boundless depth of his filial prayer, not only before he freely delivered himself up ... but even in his *last words* on the Cross, where prayer and the gift of self are but one" (2605).

God's plan of salvation, expressed most fully in the Paschal Mystery, is understood in a more profound way when it's interpreted as a series of successive gifts-of-self. Indeed, our ability to give ourselves, our ability to love others, begins with God's love (1 Jn 4:19), a love which is meant to be passed on. Because of this, we're called to love one another with a divine love, albeit in a human way (1 Jn 4:7); we're called to give ourselves in imitation of Christ. This is why the Fathers of the Second Vatican Council, influenced by Cardinal Karol Wojtyla (the future Pope St. John Paul II), taught that "Man, who is the only creature on earth which God willed for itself, cannot fully find himself except through a sincere gift of himself."[10]

All of this reveals that love, properly understood, isn't to remain the sole possession of the beloved. Like the man who buried his talents (Mt 25:15–30), we cannot bury the love we receive but instead must "invest" it in others. In this sense, the gift-of-self we receive is to be re-gifted. This means it's to be passed on to others, and through us, enable the love of God to spread. Jesus says, "I give you a new commandment: love one another. As I have loved you, so you also should love one another" (Jn 13:34). Thus, having received a gift-of-self from God, we are to gift ourselves to others. In this respect, by divine providence, we incarnate God's love through our own flesh. Though we are unworthy, God allows us the privilege of actively participating in His plan of salvation. Applied to the Establishment Hypothesis (which will be treated more fully further on), this means that God's gift-of-self is successively passed on to the apostles, and through them to their successors, the bishops. The bishops then pass this gift-of-self on to priests and deacons, who themselves pass it on to the laity. The laity, having received this gift, now pass it on to the world (figure 1). This is precisely how the mission of the Church is fulfilled and how the Mystery of Salvation unfolds.

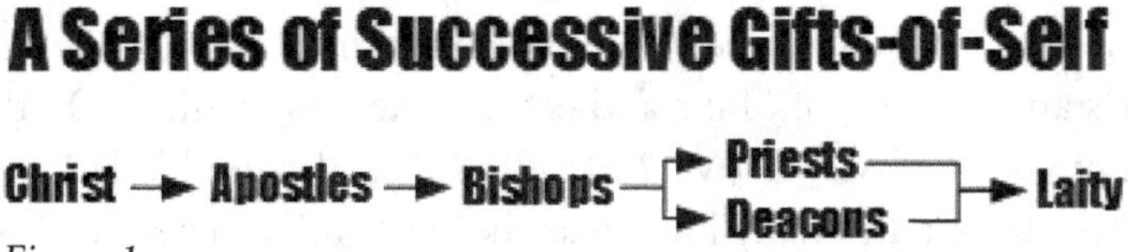

A Series of Successive Gifts-of-Self

Christ → Apostles → Bishops → [Priests, Deacons] → Laity

Figure 1

Keeping these three principles in mind, we can now turn to the Establishment Hypothesis by considering the Paschal Mystery and its relationship to the Last Supper. In many respects, the Last Supper isn't only part of the Paschal Mystery, it encapsulates it. That is to say, what Jesus said on Holy Thursday, He actually did on Good Friday — "Take ... this is my body, which will be given up for you" (Lk 22:17, 19). Indeed, by giving the command "Do this in remembrance of me" (1 Cor 11:24), He enables us to participate in the Last Supper and, by extension, the Paschal Mystery, each time Mass is celebrated. Accordingly, the *Catechism* teaches, "In the liturgy of the Church, it is principally his own Paschal Mystery that Christ signifies and makes present" (1085). In terms of the priesthood, the Church has long looked to the Last Supper as its institution (along with the episcopacy, which is the fullness of orders).[11]

If there is a cohesive unity to be found in the origins of holy orders, then it would make sense to find it in the Paschal Mystery and, because this mystery is encapsulated in the Last Supper, this event should be our starting point. As we do so, bear in mind that we're not only examining the origins of holy orders, nor are we simply exploring the nature of diaconal spirituality; rather, because of what these exemplify and reveal, we're uncovering the very basis of a lay servant spirituality. This is why considering the diaconate and the Establishment Hypothesis isn't a diversion from our primary pursuit, but the chief means by which to achieve it.

On the night before He died, Jesus shared the Passover meal with the Twelve. There, He issued two distinct sets of commands. The first, as we've already seen, is found in the Synoptic Gospels and consists of "Take and eat … Take and drink … Do this in memory of Me …" (Mt 26:17–30; Mk 14:12–26; Lk 22:7–39). These are traditionally known as the "institution narratives" because they simultaneously institute the Eucharist and the priesthood. However, during that same meal, there was another command, one not found in the Synoptics but instead only in John's Gospel. There Jesus, after washing the feet of His disciples, said, "I have given you a model to follow, so that as I have done for you, you should also do" (Jn 13:15). This command is liturgically known as the *mandatum*. On Holy Thursday, the *Ceremonial of Bishops* calls for the bishop to begin the foot washing by removing his chasuble (the outer priestly vestment), under which is his dalmatic (the outer diaconal vestment). These vestments represent the layering of Holy Orders, as the bishop's ordination to the priesthood and his subsequent ordination to the episcopacy do not supplant his earlier ordination to the diaconate. While he is bishop, he is still deacon, and the rite he is about to enact is one of service, that is to say, diaconal.

Pope Francis, during this ritual, doesn't wear the dalmatic. Instead, after removing the chasuble, he modifies his priestly stole into a diaconal stole before washing the feet of the people.[12] This is to say, he takes the stole from around his neck and refashions it to run over his left shoulder and across his chest, thus denoting a deacon. Pope Francis and the bishops do this because, while they are bishops, they still possess the diaconate, and there is something intuitively diaconal about this act.

It's fascinating to note the correlation between the two sets of commands at the Last Supper and the two elements found in the Greatest Commandment. They are, in many respects, different ways of talking about the same thing, thereby providing each with fuller meaning. Recall when the Pharisees sent a scholar of the law to test Jesus, asking Him which of the Commandments is the greatest. Recognizing their deceit, Jesus instead summarizes the Ten by saying, "You shall love the Lord, your God, with all your heart, with all your soul, and with all your mind. This is the greatest and the first commandment. The second is like it: You shall love your neighbor as yourself" (Mt 22:37-39, also: Mk 12:28-31; Lk 10:25-28; Jn 13:31-35).

According to the *Catechism*, "The Commandments take on their full meaning within the covenant" (2061). In its most basic sense, a covenant is a promissory agreement between God and humanity, either verbally or by ritual oath, that establishes a new relationship. Since the Fall (Gn 3:1-19), God has established a series of covenants with Israel as a means to slowly reconcile humanity to Himself, ever deepening His relationship with us. These are known as the old covenants, corresponding to the Old Testament. These old covenants culminate and find their fullest expression in the redemptive act of Jesus Christ, who is the New and Eternal Covenant. Whereas the Greatest Commandment represents a summary of the old covenants, the Last Supper represents the New and Everlasting Covenant (Lk 22:20), grounded in the Paschal Mystery and memorialized in the celebration of the Mass. This is expressed in all of the Eucharistic prayers when the celebrant says, "Take this, all of you and drink from it, for this is the chalice of my blood, the blood of the new and eternal covenant, which will be poured out for you and for many for the forgiveness of sins. Do this in memory of me." At the Last Supper — and in the Paschal Mystery it encapsulates — both love of God and love of neighbor are expressed respectively in the Eucharist and *mandatum*. In the Eucharist God offers His love to us through His Son Jesus Christ, making possible our ability to love Him with all of our hearts, our souls, and our minds. In a similar manner, the *mandatum* calls us to love our neighbor through service, "as I have done for you, you should also do" (Jn 13:15).

To sum things up, in the Last Supper, an event that takes up the whole of the Paschal Mystery, we have two sets of commands from Christ: One is unmistakably priestly in nature, and the other is unmistakably diaconal. In this respect, the Establishment Hypothesis isn't really new. Deacon James Keating writes, "The foot washing scene at the Last Supper is an expression of the institution of the diaconate by Christ, since it reflects the doctrinal truth of the unity of Holy Orders. There is symmetry between the '*Do this* in memory of Me' (Lk 22:19) charge to the Apostles, and his other Apostolic charge 'so that as I have done for you, *you should also do*'" (Jn 13:14–15).[13] In making this claim, Keating cites Cardinal Walter Kasper, who asserts:

> We have seen that without diaconia there cannot be a Church, because Christ himself is one who serves (Lk 22:27). Therefore, at the Last Supper ... he not only established the idea of priesthood, but, in principle, also laid the foundation of the diaconal ministry. By the washing of feet, he gave us an example, so that we also do, as he did to us (Jn 13:15). In these words, one can see the foundation of the diaconate.[14]

Where the Establishment Hypothesis breaks new ground, and where it builds upon Keating's and Kasper's intuitive observations, is that it describes precisely how this happens through a series of successive gifts-of-self (acts of love). Critical to this is the fundamental reality that we simply cannot give what we don't first possess. In other words, if the apostles hadn't received the fullness of what we now call "holy orders" from Christ, they couldn't have passed it on to the bishops. Likewise, if the bishops hadn't received holy orders from the apostles, they couldn't have passed it on to priests and deacons. In a similar fashion, if priests and deacons hadn't received their orders from the bishops, they couldn't have passed them on to the laity in the form of priestly and diaconal ministry. This progression is grounded in the Latin maxim *nemo dat quod non habet*, literally meaning, "no one gives what they don't have."

To better appreciate this progression as it relates to servant spirituality, the diaconate, and the Mystery of Salvation, I'll break this process down into seven simple steps that refer to the diagram below (figure 2). In considering these steps and the illustration that follows, it's important to notice how each step is distinguished from the others by distinct gifts-of-self that, together, form an organic continuity. Here, a step, and the group it represents, stands after the preceding step and group as a kind of emissary or envoy. Equally important is how the Establishment Hypothesis reveals that the entire Church is meant to be a servant Church and that the diaconate stands as a model and exemplar after Christ the Servant. The steps are as follows:

> **Step 1**: Through His gift-of-self on the Cross, Jesus reconciles humanity to the Father. This offer of reconciliation is encapsulated in the Last Supper, which is also a foretaste of the heavenly banquet to come.
> **Step 2**: In the Last Supper, Jesus issues two sets of commands to His apostles, one establishing the Eucharist, and the other establishing the requirement to serve.
> **Step 3**: These commands, in light of the Paschal Mystery,

establish both the priesthood through the Eucharist and the diaconate through the *mandatum* (foot washing).

Step 4: The apostles, having received this gift-of-self from Christ in the forms of the priesthood and diaconate, now gift themselves, in the forms of that same priesthood and diaconate, to their successors, the bishops.

Step 5: The bishops, having received this gift-of-self from the apostles in the forms of the priesthood and diaconate, now gift themselves to priests and deacons through the conferral of Holy Orders.

Step 6: The priests and deacons, having received this gift-of-self from the bishop in the forms of the priesthood and diaconate, now reveal in a distinctive and complementary manner the whole Christ (*Christus totus*). As a result, they gift themselves to the laity through evangelizing and the sacraments.

Step 7: The laity, having received this gift-of-self from priests and deacons, now gift themselves in the living out of their vocations for the salvation of the world.

A Spirituality Rooted in the Diaconate 59

The Establishment Hypothesis

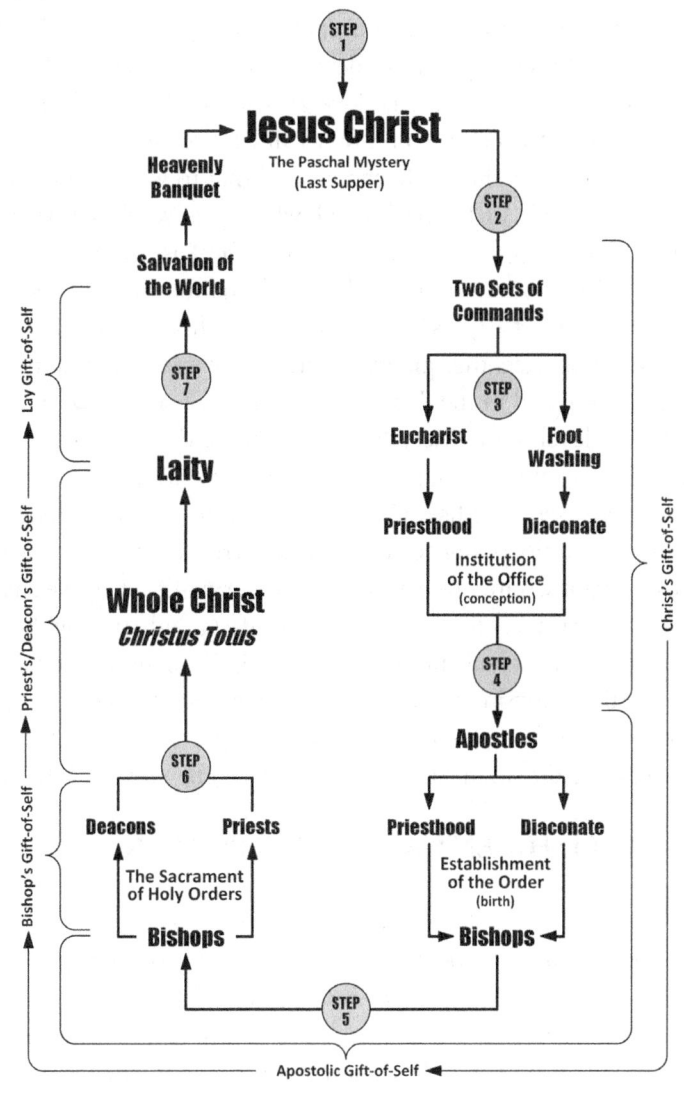

Figure 2

If the gift-of-self represents *diakonia* or service — and if this gift-of-self is the integrating theme found throughout the whole of the Mystery of Salvation — then service is central to what it means to be Church, and thus central to its spirituality. What the Establishment Hypothesis demonstrates is that service, as an outward expression of divine love, is what binds everything together. It's that which is common to all who possess holy orders by virtue of their shared diaconate, and that to which all Christians are called (Jn 13:15). Indeed, what is made clear through the successive gifts-of-self grounded in the Paschal Mystery is that Christ's priesthood (sacrifice) and His diaconate (service) find their fullest expression in the cross. This reveals that the quality of service, the quality of the gift-of-self, the quality of love is expressed in the depths of the sacrifice. Therefore, without some level of sacrifice, there is no authentic service, there is no authentic gift-of-self, there is no authentic love.

It's precisely here, having considered the origins of the diaconate and the unity of holy orders, that we arrive at the very reason for a servant Church to have a servant spirituality. If, as we shall see, our spirituality is the source of our life in faith, then without some form of servant spirituality, our faith life is diminished and our participation in the Paschal Mystery emptied of its redemptive value. It's for this reason that servant spirituality admits to a universal quality in that all of the faithful can benefit from it.

ESTABLISHMENT AND INSTITUTION

> *"Brothers, select from among you seven reputable men, filled with the Spirit and wisdom, whom we shall appoint to this task, whereas we shall devote ourselves to prayer and to the ministry of the word." The proposal was acceptable to the whole community, so they chose Stephen, a man filled with faith and the holy Spirit,*

> *also Philip, Prochorus, Nicanor, Timon, Parmenas,
> and Nicholas of Antioch, a convert to Judaism.*
> **Acts 6:3–5**

Having demonstrated the connection between the origins of holy orders, the diaconate, and servant spirituality, one more thing is needed before we can proceed. It concerns how the Establishment Hypothesis, which claims to locate the origins of the diaconate in the Paschal Mystery, can be reconciled with how these same origins have been identified in Tradition. Catholic theology admits to a certain organic unity, and therefore it's not sufficient to offer a new way of thinking without showing how it "fits" with a prior way of thinking. Tradition has long recognized, and universally affirmed, the above Scripture passage as the origins of the diaconate. The event described in it occurred after Jesus' ascension and therefore after the Last Supper. How then can we reconcile the institution of the seven deacons (as found in Acts 6:3–5) with the Establishment Hypothesis that establishes the diaconate in Christ's Paschal Mystery? Because it's grounded in Divine Revelation, the institution can't be dismissed, nor can it be diminished. It must, if the hypothesis is to maintain its integrity, be reconciled in some meaningful way, such that the institution becomes an integral part of the hypothesis.

One way to address this apparent conflict is through the distinction between *officium* (office) and *ordo* (order). Whereas an office is a position in a larger organization that carries with it a specific function (figure 2, step 3), an order is an office shared by two or more persons, who together form a recognized body (figure 2, step 4). Logically speaking, an office always precedes an order. So, for example, before someone can enter the order of bishops, there must first be an episcopal office. Similarly, before someone can enter the order of presbyters, there must first be the presbyteral office. Likewise, before someone can enter the order of deacons, there must first be a diaconal office. This distinction explains how it's possible that the *mandatum* at the Last Supper established the office of deacon, while the selection of the Seven and laying on of hands represents the institution of the diaconal order.

If this seems somewhat obscure, perhaps a simple biological analogy would be helpful. Let's consider the conception of a baby within his mother's womb, followed by his birth. While an office represents a kind of conception, an order represents a kind of birth (Figure 2, Steps 3&4). Just as conception is the coming to be of someone, the *mandatum* is the coming to be of the diaconate. Likewise, just as birth is the outward revelation of a conception, so too is the institution of the Seven the outward revelation of the *mandatum*. Such an understanding reconciles the Establishment Hypothesis with the Church's traditional teaching about the diaconate, in much the same way as conception and birth are reconciled. They aren't two distinct things; rather, they are the growth of one thing looked at from two distinct stages of development. Such an approach lends a sense of continuity and trajectory that neither of the two do alone.

There is some implicit evidence for this process in the Scriptures. We know, for example, that the office of priesthood was established at the Last Supper. However, the presbyteral order was instituted sometime after as witnessed by Luke (Acts 15:6, 23) and Peter (1 Pt 5:1). Likewise, we can say that the episcopal office (order of bishops) was also established at the Last Supper. However, the episcopal order (order of priest) was instituted sometime after as witnessed by Timothy (1 Tm 3). If this is true of the presbyterate and episcopate, then it's reasonable to conclude that it's also true of the diaconate. Folding all three degrees of holy orders into the Establishment Hypothesis provides a clearer understanding of their unity, diversity, and complementarity, while at the same time grounding them together in the Paschal Mystery.

Christ's total gift-of-self means that the complementary relationships among the episcopacy, priesthood, and diaconate find their nexus in the one person of Christ. Each order participates and contributes in a unique way, bringing the *Christus totus* to the world. This means that, through the use of Pope St. John Paul II's personalist language, we have, for the first time, not only a new way of envisioning the origins of the diaconate, but perhaps even more importantly an organic way of speaking about the unity of holy orders and its impact on servant spirituality.

If the above is true, and I believe that it is, then the diaconate isn't ancillary to God's plan of salvation, but an absolutely integral and indispensable component born in the mind of the Father before all ages. In a similar way, the laity's call to service isn't ancillary to God's plan of salvation, but like the diaconate, albeit it in a different way, an absolutely integral and indispensable component. With this in mind, we now possess a firm theological basis by which we can develop a servant spirituality as distinct from, but nonetheless related to, diaconal spirituality.

RELATIONSHIP, IDENTITY, AND MISSION

> *We should always look to God as in ourselves, no matter in what manner we meditate upon Him, so as to accustom ourselves to dwell in His Divine Presence. For when we behold Him within our souls, all our powers and faculties, and even our senses, are recollected within us. If we look at God apart from ourselves, we are easily distracted by exterior objects.*
> **Saint Margaret Mary Alacoque, Letters**

In developing a servant spirituality, it would be tempting, given the theological foundation already laid, to jump in and consider the various practical elements associated with this approach. To be sure, these practical matters will make up much of this book, but our haste at this point would result in a lack of context, and, as they say, "context is everything." By "context" I mean a simple framework that will help us understand the connection among our relationship to, identity in, and mission with Jesus Christ. Relationship, identity, and mission make up a triad with their association describing the dynamic proper to any authentic Catholic spirituality. In our case, because we're considering servant spirituality, questions concerning relationship, identity, and mission must, by necessity, be directed to Christ the Servant.

Several years back, I had the opportunity to make a retreat under the direction of Deacon James Keating. The retreat involved only two retreatants, of which I was one. It was held in Omaha during one of the summer sessions of the Institute of Priestly Formation (IPF), where Keating was the Director of Theological Formation. A central tenant of IPF is built around the principles of relationship, identity, and mission, known by the acronym RIM. It was developed by IPF's Executive Director, Fr. Richard Gabuzda, and first delivered in a paper for one of their symposiums.[15]

As Keating explained RIM and applied it to the diaconate, I was immediately captivated by its elegant simplicity. It put into words something that had stirred in my heart for many years. I knew that, like the experience of many in priestly formation, much of my diaconal formation had lacked a solid spiritual dimension. Sure, all formation programs and seminaries address spirituality, but quite often they do so in a rather external, dispassionate, and objective sense, leaving it up to seminarians and diaconal candidates to take it up with their spiritual directors. This approach seems to me grossly lacking.

As we've already seen, unlike the priesthood, which over the centuries developed a robust theology upon which to build a spirituality, the diaconate had but a rudimentary and fragmented theology. This complicated matters since all spiritualities, by their very nature, are grounded in the sources of Revelation and expressed in the Church's Tradition. Without a clear sense of what the diaconate is, and its place within the Mystery of Salvation, it's difficult to develop an authentic diaconal spirituality. Indeed, if this is true for the diaconate, then it follows, based on our earlier reflections, that this is also true for a lay version of that same spirituality. This is precisely why it was first necessary to develop a theology of the diaconate through such insights as service as a gift-of-self and the Establishment Hypothesis. From here, a diaconal spirituality could be developed, and with it a corresponding servant spirituality for the laity. While Pope St. John Paul II gave me the language to develop this theology, the IPF gave me the means by which to articulate how the spiritual life relates to identity and, equally important, how this identity is crucial to fulfilling our mission. Together, these give rise to what we can rightly call "servant spirituality." To better grasp the RIM dynamic (figure 3), and how it relates to servant spirituality, I will unpack each of these three elements.

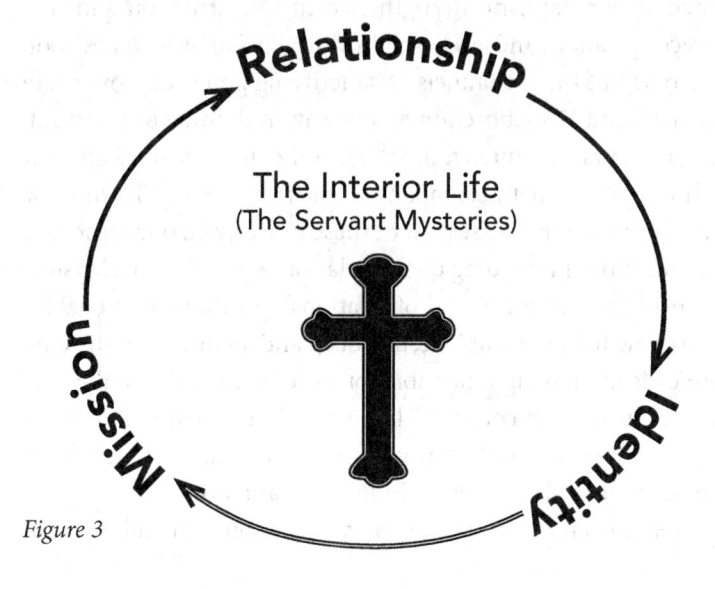

Relationship

The Interior Life
(The Servant Mysteries)

Mission   **Identity**

Figure 3

Relationship: In the above diagram, the inner part of the circle represents the interior life where, in response to our baptismal call to follow Christ, we prayerfully contemplate the Servant Mysteries. Recall that the Servant Mysteries are the revelation of Christ the Servant as He is manifested in the Scriptures, Tradition, Magisterium, and, in particular, the sacrament of the present moment — that is, in the ins and outs of our everyday life. Though this will be taken up in greater detail as we proceed, it's sufficient at this time to understand contemplation of these mysteries as the "place" of ongoing encounter with the One who calls us to Himself. As we have already seen, this call, properly understood as our vocation, isn't so much a call to something (our state in life), but an intimate call to Someone (Christ Jesus). It's an invitation to share in the inner life of the Trinity by way of our vocation and, in doing so, bear witness to Christ the Servant.

Here our witness rises and falls in direct proportion to the intimacy we share. It's precisely within this call, and our response to it, that a new relationship — begun at our creation, consecrated at our Baptism, strengthened in Confirmation, purified in reconciliation, and nourished in the Eucharist — takes root. As a result of these channels of sanctifying grace, we now relate to Christ and His Church in a new way, in the way of a servant. This, of course, requires full, active, and conscious participation with the graces that accompany these sacraments. The interior transformation that arises out of these graces, and our responses to them through ongoing contemplation of the Servant Mysteries, fosters a particular kind of relationship with God. It enables us to come to know and love, in a deep and abiding way, the One who calls us, making it possible for us to witness Christ the Servant to those we encounter. This subtle, but nonetheless powerful, form of evangelization is very effective because it incarnates Christ; it makes Him present in the here and now.

Relationship corresponds to what the spiritual and mystical

tradition calls abandonment, though the terms are not quite synonymous. Abandonment bespeaks the quality of the relationship in which one or both parties surrender their wills to the other. It's an act of love, expressed in a gift-of-self, implying full confidence that what is surrendered, while vulnerable, remains safe. Though abandonment is typically spoken of as a surrender of the will, the will, as a power of the soul, really signifies the entire person. It's the seat of our choices, which are the result of a deliberation of the intellect. Indeed, it's from the will that we manifest our very selves to the world in and through specific concrete acts. As St. Vincent Pallotti observes, "Remember that the Christian life is one of action, not of speech and daydreams. Let there be few words and many deeds and let them be done well." These deeds move the interior life to the exterior and back again. As such, to abandon the will is to surrender oneself willingly to another. Such an abandonment isn't a relinquishing of responsibility, a kind of spiritual copout, but instead a willingness to unite our will with Christ the Servant in the complete confidence that together, and only together, will our lives be fulfilled.

Abandonment, as we shall see in greater detail, isn't a single event. Rather, it's a lifelong process comprised of a series of connected events that enable us to share our life with Christ Jesus. It's precisely within this close sharing that intimacy is experienced and deepened. These events are begun in the interior life as that interior life encounters the Servant Mysteries. This could be in prayer or meditation, in ministry or at work, in being a wife or mother, husband or father, in fact, in every endeavor of life. While these present moments arise in the exterior life, when they are consciously brought into the interior life, they reveal the Servant Mysteries. These mysteries don't simply make present Christ the Servant, but reveal, in a profound way, Christ's unique and unconditional love. It's this ongoing revelation that invites us to greater abandonment and, with it, greater intimacy.

Identity: Within this relationship of abandonment, we experience the beauty that is God and are wounded at the depths of our soul. This woundedness, as we shall see, brings about a transformation such that we gain a new identity. Much like in courtship, at some point in time the two are so struck with each other that they marry. Here their relationship reaches such an intensity that it brings about a change in identity. He is now *husband*, and she is now *wife*. While they remain the same, they see and understand who they are in a fundamentally different way. The same is true with the Christian life. At some point in the discernment process the intimacy matures, requiring by a positive act of the will a choice that will forever change the person. As in marriage, this change reveals a fundamental truth — relationship gives rise to identity. Our connectedness to another shapes who we are. Thus, a wife is only a wife in relation to her husband, a husband is only a husband in relation to his wife, and a Christian is only a Christian in relation to Christ. The more intense the relationship, the greater its impact on identity. As a result, to the extent that the relationship grows or diminishes, so too does identity in direct proportion.

It's important to recognize that this new identity isn't something other than who we are. We don't become someone else, adopting foreign traits and strange ways. Rather, if the relationship is healthy, this new identity strengthens and fulfills who we already know ourselves to be. In many respects, we become more fully who we are, more fully alive. This is simply an application of grace perfecting nature. The sanctifying grace received at the reception of the sacraments comes about through an intense encounter that configures us to Christ. This grace capacitates us to rise above the effects of sin, enabling us to become what God fully intends us to be, revealing who we really are. Of this St. Thomas Aquinas asserts, "Although man is inclined to an end by nature, yet he cannot attain that end by nature, but only by grace because of the exalted character of the end."[16] Applied here, the specific kind of sanctifying grace associated with the sacraments enables the Christian to be Christian and, through that identity, realize his final end, intimate communion with the Trinity forever. It gives us a sense of who we really are. In this respect, we so identify with Christ the Servant that, in a certain sense, we become Christ the Servant by incarnating Him in our lives.

Mission: Pope St. John Paul II was fond of remarking that the Church doesn't have a mission, she *is* a mission. In his 1990 encyclical *Redemptoris Missio* he writes, "This definitive self-revelation of God is the fundamental reason why the Church is missionary by her very nature. She cannot do other than proclaim the Gospel."[17] Understood this way, mission stands at the very heart of the Church. It's her reason for being, her sole focus, and, because of this, her highest work. This work, though singular in purpose, admits to a diversity of expression. Returning again to the thought of John Paul II, he writes, "Mission is a single but complex reality, and it develops in a variety of ways."[18]

While all of the faithful belong to this mission, the laity are called to live it out in a specific way, sharing in the responsibility primarily entrusted to the clergy (CCC 1536). As the Fathers of the Second Vatican Council taught, "These faithful are by Baptism made one body with Christ and are constituted among the People of God ... they carry out for their own part the mission of the whole Christian people in the Church."[19] This unique and indispensable contribution by the laity was illustrated by the Establishment Hypothesis as not merely assisting the clergy but essentially sharing in the call of the Church to evangelize. As Pope Benedict XVI observed, the laity:

> Should not be regarded as "collaborators" of the clergy, but, rather, as people who are really "co-responsible" for the Church's being and acting. It is therefore import-

ant that a mature and committed laity be consolidated, which can make its own specific contribution to the ecclesial mission with respect for the ministries and tasks that each one has in the life of the Church and always in cordial communion with the bishops.[20]

The role of the laity, like that of the clergy, always takes place within the broader mission of the Church. It's a specific participation in, and a realization of, the call to go and make disciples of all nations (Mt 28:19). Just as the clergy shares in the Church's mission in a particular way, the laity shares in that same mission through their own vocation and state in life. Indeed, it's precisely through service — be it familial, evangelical, liturgical, catechetical, or through works of mercy — that this call to mission is carried out. While there are many ways to exercise this call, all require service as a fundamental and indispensable component. Thus, service, as described earlier, stands as the essential means by which the Church carries out her mission. Without service, without *diakonia*, the Church cannot fulfill her mandate, and Christ's passion, death, and resurrection is emptied of its saving power. In this respect, the Church can rightly be called a Servant Church. This is why the diaconate is so essential to the mission of the Church and why servant spirituality and its witness to Christ the Servant are so crucial to all who share in that very mission.

Of this Pope St. John Paul II writes, "Without witnesses there can be no witness, just as without missionaries there can be no missionary activity."[21] The mission of the Church, conveyed in her missionary activity, is realized in our witness to Christ, which finds its concrete expression in ministerial service, be it priestly, diaconal, religious, or lay. The call to bear witness to Christ the Servant by the faithful is a call to bear witness to the One who exercised the greatest act of service through His redemptive sacrifice on the cross. It's to see in that service its real meaning, a divine love outpoured. In many respects, the Paschal Mystery is the measure by which all service, all acts of love, are measured. This is precisely because it refines our understanding of service as an interpersonal reality, as a gift-of-self that wills the good of the other for the sake of the other. In doing so, it can accommodate and integrate personal suffering as a sanctifying element, elevating and transforming service to a love that is sacrificial in nature. This is nothing less than a participation in the redemptive suffering of Christ, giving our service the quality of a divine love. Service, understood this way, gives love its outward expression. It makes love "transferable," so to speak, through concrete acts that reach beyond ourselves to the hearts of those we serve. As St. Augustine of Hippo so beautifully observes, "What does love look like? It has the hands to help others. It has the feet to hasten to the poor and needy. It has eyes to see misery and want. It has the ears to hear the sighs and sorrows of men. That is what love looks like."[22]

This is not to suggest that human love can compare to divine love. Rather, it's to assert that when human love, human service, is infused with divine love, divine service, it becomes far more than it is. In this regard, mission is not effective without an ever-deepening sense of identity, precisely because this sense of identity — grounded in an ever-deepening relationship with Christ the Servant — gives rise to mission. Mission, then, is a natural consequence of identity, which itself is a natural consequence of relationship. This is the essence of RIM and why it's so essential to servant spirituality. It not only illustrates the dynamic between our interior and exterior lives, it integrates and facilitates them as well.

PUTTING IT ALL TOGETHER

Mission, as an act of divine love expressed in servant spirituality, completes the RIM circle and, at the very same time, begins it anew. This is because in the very carrying out of their mission the laity grow in intimate communion with Christ the Servant. This enriches their relationship with Him which, in turn, deepens their identity, rendering their mission even more effective. The same is true, for example, in marriage. When a couple engages in their mission of a shared life — resolving conflicts, raising children, etc. — they grow in greater intimacy. That increased intimacy enhances the relationship which, in turn, deepens their identity as husband and wife, rendering their mission even more effective. In this respect, RIM takes on the characteristics of a spiral staircase, ascending each time we go around, slowly but steadily bringing us to our final destination. Thus, far from being a static once-around-the-circle reality, RIM is a dynamic that can continue throughout the life of the faithful. By integrating the interior and exterior aspects of our lives, it enables us to continually discover, in the here and now, the Servant Mysteries. It capacitates us, through grace, to incarnate these mysteries, revealing Christ the Servant, and in the very process fulfill our mission.

Beyond this, RIM provides a corrective to what can best be called *the rush to mission*. This rush arises out of a culture that places too much emphasis on functionality and too little on relationships, often reducing human beings to human doings. If, for instance, the pastor wants more extraordinary ministers of the Eucharist for Mass, we typically put an announcement in the bulletin, have a night or two of training on the functionality of dispensing our Eucharistic Lord, and then just assign ministers to various Masses. Little to no thought is given to the lay minister's relationship with or identity in Christ, often rendering their ministry void of the transformative power it possesses. Indeed, in its extreme, this way of formation serves not to draw them to greater intimacy with the One who calls them to minister, but instead allows them to hide behind what they do. The ministry itself becomes the primary way of relating to Christ, such that the spiritual life is reduced to the function of the ministry.

By reducing ministry to the thing being done, ministers don't have to render themselves vulnerable, they don't have to open up to Christ. All they have to do is punch their "piety ticket" by doing the ministry and then going home. This is not to undermine the value of service as a participation in the mission of the Church; it's only to assert that, without relationship and identity, the value of that service remains superficial. God does not want our doing. He wants our being and, if we surrender our being to Him (relationship), He elevates and transforms us (identity) and, because of this, infuses our ministry with divine love (mission). As the psalmist says, "For you do not desire sacrifice or I would give it; / a burnt offering you would not accept. / My sacrifice, O God, is a contrite spirit; / a contrite, humbled heart, O God, you will not scorn" (Ps 51:18–19). At the risk of being redundant, ministry then, as a participation in the mission of the Church, is the result of something more profound — relationship and identity. Consequently, without these two prior elements, mission is undermined and with it the very Gospel it seeks to proclaim.

MEDITATIONS AND REFLECTIONS

As discussed in the Introduction, this final section is designed to allow a deeper, more personal absorption of the material just covered. It consists of a set of two interrelated spiritual exercises, whose sole purpose is to reengage the key themes in this chapter so as to internalize the truths they contain. This approach is based on the fundamental conviction that by prayerfully reflecting and meditating on these truths, God wants to speak to you in a way that will draw you into a deeper, more intimate communion with Christ the Servant. Each exercise should begin with at least a minute or two of relaxed silence, disposing your heart to the encounter. This should be followed by either a short extemporaneous prayer or, if you choose, the following:

> *Heavenly Father, I open my heart up to You so that, through the power of Your most Holy Spirit, I may encounter Your Son, Christ the Servant, in a deeply personal and transformative way. Forgive my sins and free me from the attachments of this world so that I am better attentive to Your presence and, in this attentiveness, hear what You want me to hear. Give me the grace to abandon myself to You in this moment, for, in the depths of my soul, I want nothing more than You. Speak, Lord, Your servant listens. Mary, Mother of Christ the Servant, pray for me. Amen.*

KEY THEMES

The following represent some key themes found in this chapter. As you reflect on them, consider what Christ the Servant is revealing about Himself and, more importantly, what He's revealing about you. In this you're asking two distinct but related questions: Lord, what are You saying *in general* and, flowing from this, what are You saying specifically *to me*. Ponder how what is said may impact your relationship to Him, and how this may influence your relationship with others, particularly in the choices you make. Remember, as you meditate upon these things, to write down your thoughts in your journal or spiritual notebook. This may be a single word, a sentence, a paragraph, or even more. The purpose here is to capture the most important elements of your meditation, even if they are not whole or complete.

As noted earlier, what is offered in these exercises is by way of a pious recommendation. You are free to fully engage or completely omit them as you see fit. Should you decide to move forward, you may take on one, some, or even all of the themes as the Spirit prompts you. This exercise and its effectiveness rely on grace and your openness to that grace. With all of this in mind, the key themes are as follows:

- The relationship between diaconal spirituality and servant spirituality
- Service as a gift-of-self that wills the good of the other for the sake of the other
- Servants as envoys or emissaries of divine love
- The Establishment Hypothesis
- The role of the laity in the Mystery of Salvation
- The RIM Dynamic

REFLECTION QUESTIONS

Now that you have meditated upon these themes and captured what Christ the Servant may be saying to you, you can explore them further in the following six reflection questions. It's recommended that this be done in a separate sitting, giving you a chance to digest the fruit of your initial meditation. If you do choose to turn to the reflection questions in a separate sitting, begin again with silence and prayer as described above. As with the key themes, write down your insights and thoughts in your journal or spiritual notebook.

- Identify two or three things you learned from this chapter that you didn't know before.
- Identify two or three key insights you gained through this chapter into your spiritual life, family, God, or the Church.
- Identify two or three ideas to apply your learning and insights from this chapter to your life as a Catholic.
- How might reading this chapter and reflecting on the key themes found within it deepen your *rela-*

76 Discovering Christ the Servant

tionship to Christ the Servant?
- How might reading this chapter and reflecting on the key themes found within it deepen your *identity in Christ the Servant*?
- How might reading this chapter and reflecting on the key themes found within it deepen your *mission with Christ the Servant*?

Chapter Two
The Centrality of the Spiritual Life

What more do you want, O soul! And what else do you search for outside, when within yourself you possess your riches, delights, satisfactions, fullness, and kingdom — your Beloved whom you desire and seek? Be joyful and gladdened in your interior recollection with Him, for you have Him so close to you. Desire Him there, adore Him there.
Saint John of the Cross, *Spiritual Canticle*

Having laid the theological groundwork for a servant spirituality, it's now time to consider what is often taken for granted: the centrality of the spiritual life. I say "taken for granted" because, in most adult faith formation programs, the spiritual life is assumed rather than addressed; or, if it's addressed, it's addressed in a limited manner, minimizing its significance. This is also true, though to a lesser extent, in Scripture studies and prayer groups. Using RIM language, what is often missing are relationship and identity. Rarely do such groups address the participant's interior life and the identity that springs from it. While there are some exceptions, emphasis in these programs is generally placed almost entirely on mission. To better appreciate what I mean here, consider that the primary purpose of catechesis isn't (or shouldn't be) to make the faithful more knowledgeable about Church teaching, as good and noble as that is. Rather, catechesis is ultimately about falling in love with Jesus Christ. As Pope St. John Paul II taught, "the definitive aim of catechesis is to put people not only in touch but in communion, in intimacy, with Jesus Christ: only He can lead us to the love of the Father in the Spirit and make us share in the life of the Holy Trinity."[1] Knowledge about the Scriptures, Tradition, and the Magisterium are essential means to a final end, the cultivation of the interior life, which is precisely where intimate communion takes place.

As we've seen, any consideration of a servant spirituality (or for that matter, the consideration of any spirituality), if it's to be effective, must start with the RIM dynamic. It must start with relationship, and that relationship, by necessity, is predicated upon the centrality of the spiritual life. Without this starting point, *relationship with* Christ the Servant is constrained, *identity in* Christ the Servant is obscured, and *mission with* Christ the Servant is diminished. With this principle firmly established, we will begin our examination by exploring such topics as interiority as a place of encounter, the distinctiveness of servant spirituality, struggle in the spiritual life, and the role of grace, along with the notion of abandonment. These by no means exhaust what can be said of the primacy of the interior life as a follower of Christ. Rather, they represent key topics essential to servant spirituality and, for our purposes, offer a general overview. That said, they are sufficient to provide the reader with what is necessary to adopt a servant spirituality and, in the process, whet the appetite for other spiritual writings.

THE INTERIOR LIFE AS A PLACE OF ENCOUNTER

Ours is not so much an outward search for God, as a desire to discover Him from within. The God who created us, who loved us into being, who died for us while we were still sinners, is already present in the interior life, waiting patiently to be encountered and reencountered. While He's certainly present in the world around us — in the people we meet, in the situations we confront — that outward presence will go largely unnoticed, and be unappreciated, without an inward recognition. Our ability to see Christ in those we serve begins with an interior life attuned to His Divine Presence.

It's only in the interior life where we come to know and love Christ the Servant. As expressed succinctly in the first lesson of the *Baltimore Catechism*, knowing and loving are absolute preconditions for serving Him. This is because we simply can't love whom we don't know. Knowing isn't merely to understand God — to the extent possible — on an intellectual level through the study of the Faith, though this is essential. Without exposure to and immersion in such sources as the Scriptures, Tradition, and the Magisterium, we couldn't speak the name of Christ, much less know Him. However, to truly know Him is to move in, through, and beyond this study (which is a lifetime endeavor), to a deep, interpersonal relationship, sharing in His very life. This is only possible through the cultivation of an interior life.

Relationships, if they are healthy, are always mutual. This is to say that they admit to a kind of reciprocity that ought to grow in intimacy and tenderness over time. In deepening our relationship with God through perfection in the spiritual life, we come, ever so slowly at first, to see ourselves as God sees us, albeit in a limited way. This wondrous self-revelation enables us to begin to appreciate our real self-worth. We are, as Jesus demonstrated so beautifully on the cross, someone worth dying for. Entering into this truth helps us to see that everything we have, every event we experience, be they triumphs or tragedies, is a gift from God.

When we prayerfully reflect on these gifts, when we meditate upon their implications, we discover in and through them the Giver — we encounter none other than God Himself. These gifts are, in many respects, sacramental. They enable us, in a certain sense, to transcend the material world to the spiritual, and there abide in His saving presence. Here, as we bask in the light of His love, we're overwhelmed by the encounter and experience a profound sense of gratitude. "Lord, I am not worthy to have you enter under my roof" (Mt 8:8). It's precisely this gratitude, born of our participation in divine love, that is the inspiration of, and motivation for, a life lived in faith. Thus, the source of our life and ministry, that which enables us to effectively incarnate Christ the Servant in the living out of our vocations, is nothing other than intimate communion with Him. The interior life represents the place of inner encounter with Christ, without which we are blind to the many exterior encounters that come our way each day. This inner encounter is that which transforms what we do from a mundane act to a saving reality.

In its broadest sense, the interior life is that inner place where we're alone with ourselves. It's the place of thought, imagination, deliberation, and choice. It's where we dream, pray, reflect, and meditate. It's where we discover God, ourselves, and others. It's the inner space where truth is grasped, goodness is acquired, beauty is appreciated, and love is born.

It's possible, with some reflection, to distinguish between the various dimensions of the interior life. There's the speculative, capable of intellectual thought; the moral, capable of choosing good or evil; and the spiritual, capable of intimacy with God and others. These, of course, are interrelated and, in a certain sense, interpenetrate one another, finding their nexus in our one person. Although they can be distinguished by their operations, they can't be separated without somehow obscuring the whole person.

While the interior life admits to these dimensions, when we speak of it we tend to speak of the spiritual dimension. Because of this, terms such as interiority, the inner life, and the spiritual life are often used synonymously in the Church's Tradition. For our purpose, we will follow this usage, with all of these terms referring to that inner place where we encounter Christ and seek intimate communion with Him.

The interior life is nonphysical and, because of this, finds its exercises within the powers of the soul. To be human is to be a body/soul composite, and while the soul expresses the interior life, the body expresses the exterior life. These two aspects of our human nature are to be integrated. This integrity requires that, for the interior life to be authentically lived, it must be expressed in the exterior life. This is nothing less than a corollary of faith and works. Accordingly, Saint James writes:

> What good is it, my brothers, if someone says he has faith but does not have works? Can that faith save him? If a brother or sister has nothing to wear and has no food for the day, and one of you says to them, "Go in peace, keep warm, and eat well," but you do not give them the necessities of the body, what good is it? So also faith of itself, if it does not have works, is dead. ... For just as a body without a spirit is dead, so also faith without works is dead. (James 2:14–17, 26)

Faith is an act of the interior life. For it to be realized and lived, it must be expressed in concrete acts consistent with what is professed. To do otherwise is to undermine its authenticity and integrity, calling into question whether that faith is truly held by the one professing it. Thus, if someone were to profess to be a faithful Catholic while, at the same time, being unfaithful to his wife, his profession of faith would be significantly undercut by his actions. Indeed, those actions that are inconsistent with his faith would call into question whether he truly believes what he says he believes. He may deceive others, and even himself, but his inconsistency reveals not his fidelity, but his infidelity. Beyond this, if he freely and willingly engages in what he knows to be grave matter, he breaks communion with God and His Church. This is hardly the act of a faithful Catholic.

In many respects, the relationship between the interior and exterior life is sacramental. Properly understood, sacramentals, like the sacraments themselves, are visible signs of invisible realities. The sign points to and makes present that which is hidden. Just as the body is the sacrament of the soul, the exterior life is a sacrament of the interior life. Without the body, the soul remains unknown, trapped in the realm of the spirit. It's precisely in and through the body that the soul enters the world, makes itself known, and, equally important, comes to be known. Together, and only together, do body and soul express the whole person. In a similar manner, without the exterior life, the interior remains unknown. It's strictly in and through the exterior life that the interior life is revealed. Together, and only together, do they express the whole person.

To share such things as faith and spirituality, hopes and aspirations — indeed, our very selves in love — the interior life must transcend itself. This only takes place through the exterior life, expressed in concrete acts. Likewise, to receive another's faith and spirituality, hopes and aspirations — indeed, his or her very self in love — only occurs first through our exterior life. Our interior life is only accessed through the exterior life. This intrinsic relationship means that, while we can explore servant spirituality, we do so with the understanding that, like faith and works, the interior life without the exterior life is dead.

THE DISTINCTIVENESS OF A SPIRITUALITY OF SERVICE

> *If you are what you should be, you will set the whole world ablaze!*
> **Adapted from St. Catherine of Sienna's Letter to Stefano Maconi**

When the phrase *servant spirituality* is used, its meaning might be assumed from the combination of its two terms. They imply the way we draw close to Christ the Servant is through such practices as *lectio divina,* various devotions, spiritual direction, frequent confession, and Eucharistic adoration. While all of these have great merit in cultivating the interior life, in themselves they don't constitute a servant spirituality as such, but instead are elements of a servant spirituality. This may seem like a distinction without a difference, but upon closer examination the difference is vast.

To be sure, we may and should participate in these various devotions; yet, as we shall see, it's not the fact of our participation, but rather how we participate, that reflects our intimacy with Christ the Servant. All of these devotions are a way of relating to God, and that relationship changed radically on the day of our Baptism. Because we are Christian, because we have been indelibly marked as belonging to Christ the Servant, we now have the capacity of relating to God in a particular way, in a servant way. Since this relationship is contextualized as a gift of divine love outpoured, and since love cannot remain static, the essential characteristic and distinctive feature of servant spirituality is to grow in more intimate communion with Christ the Servant. In many respects, this not only defines servant spirituality but defines us, and it becomes the source and strength of our life and faith. It imbues our vocation with a particular quality, the quality of a servant who loves the Master tenderly.

The above definition, which forms the basis of our approach, uses the term *servant spirituality* in a collective sense: What is really meant is "servant spiritualities." There's not any one way to grow in intimate communion with Christ the Servant, but many. Indeed, what is true of servant spiritualities, and their associated devotions, is true of all Catholic spiritualities. In his venerable work *Introduction to the Devout Life*, St. Francis de Sales observes:

> When God created the world, He commanded each tree to bear fruit after its kind; and even so He bids Christians, the living trees of His Church, to bring forth fruits of devotion, each one according to his kind and vocation. A different exercise of devotion is required of each ... and furthermore such practice must be modified according to the strength, the calling, and the duties of each individual.[2]

As we have already seen, intimate communion implies a relationship, and a relationship always implies the union of two or more distinct individuals. While Christ the Servant is a constant in the relationship, individuals are not. They represent a widely diverse group and, while there are many commonalities among them, the manner in which they encounter Christ, and allow Him to accompany them on their vocational journeys, will differ. Just as no one person can image God completely, so no one person can incarnate Christ the Servant completely. The diversity of servant spiritualities reflects the diversity of the People of

God, and only together do they reveal Christ the Servant. In this way, they enable their lives and faith to permeate and penetrate all aspects of society. Thus, what will be considered in this work is that which is common to all servant spiritualities, along with ways to cultivate their growth.

The uniqueness of a servant spirituality, what sets it apart from other spiritualities, lies in a mystical identification with Christ the Servant. While all are called to serve by virtue of their Baptism, the deacon is called to be an icon of Christ the Servant and, in this respect, he acts in the person of that same Christ who came not to be served, but to serve. His witness, his diaconal spirituality, ought to provide the laity with a preeminent example of servant spirituality. Both diaconal spirituality and its lay form, servant spirituality, are grounded in a specific kind of vocational relationship to God. It's a relationship that begins as an unfulfilled calling, beckoning each person to a life lived in sacred service each according to his or her own vocation and state in life. For the deacon, it's realized when his bishop says the prayer of ordination and lays hands upon him. It continues throughout his life as he exercises his diaconal ministry. Because he *is deacon* by virtue of his ordination, every act that proceeds from him has the capacity to be diaconal. I say "has the capacity" because the deacon needs to be intentional about being a deacon. In a similar way, for the laity, it's realized in their Baptism and in the laying of hands by the bishop in Confirmation. It continues throughout their lives as they live out their Catholic faith. Because they've been marked by Christ the Servant in Baptism and Confirmation, every act that proceeds from them has the capacity to be one of sacred service. I say "has the capacity" because they need to be intentional about being a servant in Christ.

Servant spirituality, in its many forms, seeks to grow us in the ways of perfection, enabling us to incarnate Christ the Servant more effectively as husbands and wives, mothers and fathers, brothers and sisters, friends and neighbors. By sensitizing us to God's presence in those we serve, and responding in love, we extend the hand of Christ to those in need. In this very process, we're transformed, since it's impossible to touch without being touched. To foster a greater intentionality within the exercise of our lives, we need to foster that same intentionality within the interior life. We need to seek Christ the Servant in all things and, in all things, discover Him anew.

THE IMPORTANCE OF EMPATHY

> *We should be cordial and affable with the poor, and with persons in humble circumstances. We should not treat them in a supercilious manner. Haughtiness makes them revolt. On the contrary, when we are affable with them, they become more docile and derive more benefit from the advice they receive.*
> **St. Vincent de Paul**

To serve others is to perceive a need in them and, to the extent possible, help them satisfy that need. If it's hunger, we give them food. If it's faith, we proclaim the Good News. If it's loneliness, we give them company. Sometimes this means doing something, most times it just means being present. In either case, our sensitivity to the needs of others, and consequently the desire to serve, arises not so much from a particular situation, but first and foremost in our interiority. It's here where we feel another's pain, experiencing, albeit in a limited sense, his or her suffering. This servant characteristic has, as its basis, the virtue of empathy. Because empathy is critical to authentic Christian service, and because Christians are meant to exemplify service and inspire others to serve, empathy is essential to an authentic servant spirituality. Without it, we cannot serve as Christ served. Without it, we cannot reach beyond our own limitations into the depths of those who suffer, providing the strength and consolation they so desperately need.

In its most basic sense, empathy concerns the ability to recognize and enter into the experience of another. The term is grounded in the Greek prefix *em* meaning "in" and the word *pathos* meaning "suffering." This implies a deep personal sharing in another's hardship, such that the one empathizing experiences, in a certain sense, the hardship of the other. Empathy creates a bond between the two — the one accompanying the other as he carries his cross, reminding him that he's not alone and that someone cares. It is, in this respect, nothing less than an act of love.

In servant spirituality, it's important to recognize that the object of authentic empathy is not so much the suffering of the other but the other himself. Empathy is, at its core, an interpersonal reality. In this regard, by being empathetic, we accompany the sufferer through his or her sufferings. This may seem, in a world dominated by positive action, to be feeble and ineffective. To sit by a hospital bed, or to spend time with someone with mental illness, or to simply visit a person who has lost a loved one may seem rather futile considering the sickness, illness, or loss itself. However, a comforting presence — one which takes on the suffering of the other by just being there and listening quietly — brings a consolation that enables the sufferer not only to endure, but to rise above the hardship, experiencing its redemptive value. Jesus is the perfect model of empathy. By virtue of his Incarnation, He enters into the human condition with all of its sufferings. Not content to be a bystander dispassionately removed from human pathos, He takes on humanity's suffering through His passion and death. Notice how Our Lord exercises this priestly aspect of His earthly ministry in a preeminently diaconal way, in a way that exemplifies Christian service.

In his book *The Heart of the Diaconate*, Deacon James Keating writes, "Empathy will only remain and deepen over many decades of ecclesial service if that empathy is sourced in Christ and restored in Him when human strength, interest and generosity lag."[3] This is as true for the laity as it is for the deacon. While the fullness of God's grace subsists in the Catholic Church,[4] the finite Church cannot contain the infinite nature of God's grace. We see this in the many examples of the noble atheist, whose selfless altruism inspires others. Nonetheless, it's often the case that love-of-man, without the corresponding love-of-God, renders the noble atheist incapable of sourcing his love beyond himself. True, his love is ultimately a limited participation in divine love, but it's rooted in a God he does not know, and so he cannot draw from Him, be inspired by Him, or be strengthened in Him.

However, when we root our spirituality and life in the love of Christ the Servant, we grow to understand empathy in light of the Paschal Mystery and its personal promise of salvation. This broader spiritual approach enables us to appreciate empathy from Calvary to the empty tomb. It understands that empathy is often more about being at the foot of the cross with the one who suffers, awaiting the resurrection together, rather than "doing something." This being-with the sufferer is not the absence of love but, many times, is the very best kind of love.

Like other spiritualities in the Church, servant spirituality doesn't arise in a vacuum. Rather, it's contextualized and enriched by a diverse spiritual, mystical, and ascetical tradition. When oriented to intimate communion with Christ the Servant, this tradition provides the necessary building blocks from which an authentic servant spirituality is developed and maintained. With that in mind, we would do well to begin with what is one of the chief hallmarks of any spirituality: interior struggle. Treating this early in our consideration allows us the ability to anticipate it and, when it rears its ugly head, to cut it off by responding to God's grace.

STRUGGLE IN THE SPIRITUAL LIFE

> *The struggle is the sign of holiness. A saint is a sinner that keeps trying ... Our interior life consists in beginning again and again.*
> **Saint Josemaría Escrivá, *Christ Is Passing By***

The interior life is both a gift from God and an intentional response on our part. In the midst of life's demands, this response often requires great effort to sustain. As a result, if we're to progress in the spiritual life, we must consider, as an essential component, the struggles that accompany it. By struggles, I mean the ongoing work associated with picking up our cross and following Jesus. This includes the difficulties associated with various forms of prayer, meditations, devotions, or spiritual practices as they relate to the living out of our vocations. In many respects, to pray well is to struggle often. As the entire Tradition bears witness, the two go hand-in-hand.

To identify the spiritual life as a struggle is to beg some deeper questions, the first of which concerns the reason for our struggle. Why do we struggle? Much of this has to do with the effects of what Tradition calls "the three enemies of the soul" — the world, the flesh, and the devil. These are the sources of our temptation, and they arise in a world tainted by original sin and still awaiting full redemption. They mirror Christ's temptations in the desert found in all three Synoptic Gospels (Mt 4:1–11; Mk 1:12–13; Lk 4:1–13). The world is represented by casting Our Lord off the pinnacle, the flesh by turning stones into bread, and the devil by worshiping Satan. Elements of this triad can also be found in the Parable of the Sower (Mt 13:1–23; Mk 4:1–20; Lk 8:4–15) and in Saint Paul's Letter to the Ephesians where he writes, "All of us once lived among them in the desires of our flesh, following the wishes of the flesh and the impulses, and we were by nature children of wrath, like the rest" (Eph 2:3, see also verse 2).

THE UNHOLY TRINITY AND SLOTH

> *O Lord and Master of my life, grant me not a spirit*
> *of sloth, meddling, love of power, and idle talk. But*
> *give to me, your servant, a spirit of sober-mindedness,*
> *humility, patience, and love. Yes, O Lord and King,*
> *grant me to see my own faults and not to judge my*
> *brother, since you are blessed to the ages of ages. Amen.*
> **The Great Lenten Prayer of Saint Ephrem,**
> **Byzantine and Orthodox Traditions**

Reflecting on temptation in light of the moral life, Tradition summarized these enticements to sin, giving them the popular title the "Unholy Trinity." Accordingly, the French medieval philosopher Peter Abelard identified three specific categories of temptation as the world, the flesh, and the devil. Likewise, St. Thomas Aquinas acknowledged the deadly nature of these in his *Summa Theologica*. Later, St. John of the Cross identified these very same three as serious threats to the perfection of the soul. Although the definitions and treatments given by these thinkers vary slightly, they are, for the most part, quite consistent in their understanding.

The *world* represents a willful indifference to the designs of God. This can be seen in the adoption of secular values in opposition to Christ and His Church. An example of the "world" is what Pope St. John Paul II called "the culture of death," which includes the widespread acceptance of contraception, abortion, infanticide, and euthanasia. The *flesh* reflects the tendencies to gluttony and sexual immorality. These include our disordered passions and corrupt inclinations expressed in such evils as fornication, adultery, and homosexual acts. The *devil* represents himself — he is a real person, the chief fallen angel described by Saint John as the liar and the father of lies (Jn 8:44; 1 Jn 3:8). He, along with the rest of the fallen angels known as demons, "prowl throughout the world seeking the ruin of souls."[5] Examples of the "devil" include such deadly practices as openness to temptation, participation in the occult, and satanism. When embraced or even passively tolerated, the Unholy Trinity can have the real potential to erode our relationship with Christ the Servant, significantly diminishing our participation in the Faith and, if left unchecked, contribute to the loss of our salvation.

These threats, often experienced in the form of strong temptations, represent the prime reason for struggle in the interior life. Others include what Tradition calls the seven deadly sins, which actually fall under the broader categories of the world, the flesh, and the devil. They are pride, greed, lust, envy, gluttony, wrath, and sloth. While treatment of these can be found in a number of good sources (CCC 1866),[6] one of these capital sins stands out as particularly troublesome in the spiritual life: that of sloth.

Sloth, also referred to by its Greek word *acedia*, refers to an interior struggle characterized by indifference to our religious duties and obligations. It's a kind of spiritual malaise where we fail to do the things we should. In this respect, it can easily become a sin of omission, especially when we cease to resist it. Writing in his *Pocket Catholic Dictionary*, the late Jesuit theologian Fr. John Hardon defined sloth as the "sluggishness of soul or boredom because of the exertion necessary for the performance of a good work."[7] Sloth arises out of the interior desire to seek pleasure and avoid hardship without regard to the moral and spiritual implications. As a result, we all too often follow the path of least resistance, becoming, in the spiritual life, nominally active and, in its extreme, religiously apathetic.

Sloth, which is as old as religion itself, was first identified as such by Evagrius of Pontus, a Desert Father in the late fourth century. Writing in the early monastic tradition, he described it as a deep desire for monks to leave their cells, arising out of an ongoing indifference to the Faith. This, in turn, easily led to futility in their monastic vocation. St. Thomas Aquinas later described it as "a sadness arising from the fact that the good is difficult."[8] Here, we become lukewarm to the promptings of the Holy Spirit, yielding to the weight of our lives and failing to source our strength in Christ the Servant.

While the laity are not monks, the same principles apply. They can allow themselves to become slothful in the spiritual life, especially when it comes to things like praying regularly and frequenting the Sacrament of Reconciliation. It's all too easy to rationalize away such spiritual exercises because of the demands of our vocation, without recognizing that unless we ground ourselves in these practices we cannot truly fulfill our vocation. In much the same way respiration requires for its success a twofold act, breathing in and breathing out, so too does the Christian life. Through the cultivation of the spiritual life, we breathe in the love of God. That same love of God, now transformed in us, is given to those we serve by breathing out. If we simply breathe in and stop, we will inevitably die. Likewise, if we simply breathe out and stop, we will also perish. This movement from interiority to exteriority and back again reveals a wholesome integrity that gives life to us, and through us to those we serve. It's also key in understanding that servant spirituality is expressed in the exterior life (our service) and is sourced in our interior life (prayer, meditation, and the sacraments).

Although, in a strict sense, sloth is often associated with inactivity, there is a type of sloth that masks itself in a flurry of actions unrelated to the interior life. As Evagrius pointed out, we may well be busy with a great many things, even holy things, and still be slothful. This happens when we busy ourselves with exterior acts of ministry as a way to avoid the much harder work associated with cultivating the interior life. Indeed, it's quite possible to hide behind our works believing that, because we exercise this ministry or that, we are exempt from the labor that accompanies growth in the spiritual life. This "ticket punching" mentality leaves the practitioner spiritually empty and, in its most extreme, like "whitewashed tombs" (Mt 23:27).

A lack of interiority associated with exterior acts leaves them, as we have already seen, sterile and lifeless. Because we fail to grow in intimacy with Christ the Servant through constancy in the interior life, sloth leads to a cold, depersonalized life in which, instead of relating to those we serve, we merely function. This is simply the consequence of our failure to encounter Jesus in the world within us; so, as a result, we're rendered incapable of recognizing Him in the world around us. This condition, and its after-effect, is poetically captured in the Book of Proverbs and its consideration of a slothful person or "sluggard." There, the sacred author writes:

> I passed by the field of a sluggard,
> by the vineyard of one with no sense;
> It was all overgrown with thistles;
> its surface was covered with nettles,
> and its stone wall broken down.
> As I gazed at it, I reflected;
> I saw and learned a lesson:
> A little sleep, a little slumber,
> a little folding of the arms to rest —
> Then poverty will come upon you like a robber,
> and want like a brigand. (24:30–34)

In examining the struggles associated with the interior life, we've considered the most common kinds of difficulties. However, if we're not careful we risk passing over that which is so obvious as to be missed. In its consideration of the battle of prayer, the *Catechism* focuses on the object of that battle when it teaches:

> Prayer is both a gift of grace and a determined response on our part. It always presupposes effort. The great figures of prayer of the Old Covenant before Christ, as well as the Mother of God, the saints, and he himself, all teach us this: prayer is a battle. Against whom? Against ourselves and against the wiles of the tempter who does all he can to turn man away from prayer, away from union with God. We pray as we live, because we live as we pray. If we do not want to act habitually according to the Spirit of Christ, neither can we pray habitually in his name. The "spiritual battle" of the Christian's new life is inseparable from the battle of prayer. (2725)

Sometimes that which is right in front of us is most hidden. With regard to the interior life, we are the only element that's constant in absolutely every single one of our struggles. Such struggles as the Unholy Trinity and sloth are made possible only by our willingness to accept them, to appropriate them, to make them our own. True, we're surrounded by things and persons that constantly tempt us, but grace in each and every one of these moments makes it not only possible to resist, but possible to use these very same temptations as spiritual "springboards" to perfection. By not recognizing ourselves as the origin of our interior struggles, we look away from the source of the problem and, at the very same time, the solution.

GRACE AS A REMEDY

> *Never give up prayer, and should you find dryness and difficulty, persevere in it for this very reason. God often desires to see what love your soul has, and love is not tried by ease and satisfaction.*
> **St. John of the Cross, *Special Counsels: Degrees of Perfection #9***

Grace is nothing less than supernatural help and, in this respect, represents an expression of divine love. To detach love from grace is to depersonalize the gift and, by extension, the Giver. Here, grace is not so much something given as Someone encountered in an intimate way. It is Christ the Servant, meeting us on the road to Calvary, helping us to carry our cross, enabling us to endure our sufferings and, in the end, to bask in the light of our own resurrection. This divine love, given to us in grace to engage in the struggles of the interior life, can never be understated. It means that God desires us more than we can ever desire Him. He seeks us out more than we seek Him. God's absolute and unconditional love, and the grace that flows from it, is most fully expressed in the passion, death, and resurrection of His Son. Jesus says, "No one has greater love than this, to lay down one's life for one's friends" (Jn 15:13).

Our Lord gives Himself to us, and in this very giving He offers the grace necessary to overcome our struggles. Because of this unconditional love, there's nothing we can do to make Him love us more, and nothing we can do to make Him love us less. He is Love through and through. With this in mind, it's a grand lie of Satan that we must be good to allow God to draw close to us. As Saint Paul observes, "God proves his love for us in that while we were still sinners Christ died for us" (Rom 5:8). We often buy into Satan's lie because we superimpose the frailties of human love over God's love, rather than allowing God's love to be the measure of our love. God's love is meant to purify our love so that our love reflects, albeit in a human way, His love. So intense is God's love for us that Saint Augustine remarks in his *Confessions*, "God love each of us as if there is only one of us."

Since it's an expression of divine love, grace is completely unmerited. There's absolutely nothing we can do to earn it. It's a gratuitous gift from God just because He's God and we're us. That's it. God's love for us is grounded not in what we do, but simply in our very being, in the pure and simple fact that we exist in His image. If this seems rather abstract, think of the love a father has for his son. Should the son, as he grows, engage in acts of which the father disapproves, such disapproval does not diminish the love he has for his son. This is nothing less than the principle of loving the sinner and hating the sin. The father sees beyond his son's acts to the babe he held long ago, to the boy he raised, to the man he's become. The father loves the son for who he is, and it's because of this love that he hates what his son's sins do to him and to others around him. Nonetheless, the father can no more abandon his son than he can abandon himself. In this respect, authentic love, be it divine or human, admits to a kind of constant, regardless of the acts of the beloved. This is not to say that human love has the same power as divine love, only that human love, when sourced in God's love, has power beyond itself. In this respect, human love, at its best, is a participation in and expression of divine love.

SURRENDER IS ABANDONMENT

> *Love consumes us only in the measure*
> *of our self-surrender.*
> **St. Thérèse of Lisieux, *The Story of a Soul***

If we accept God's help, we accept a kind of divine embrace. We allow Jesus to place His arms around us, steadying us when we falter, picking us up when we collapse, and carrying us when we're exhausted. In doing so, His strength becomes our strength, His love becomes our love, diminishing the interior struggle and rendering our life and ministry more effective. This divine help requires one thing and one thing only: that we surrender to Christ the Servant. It consists of letting go and letting God, not just in situations that exceed our strength but, eventually, in all things. Here, we don't step out of the way and passively hope God steps in, but allow Him to work in and through us, transforming us in the process. Implicit in this surrender is the recognition that we simply can't make it in this world to our eternal destiny without Him. Christ the Servant, in the hearts of the faithful, fills a space within us that no one else can fill — such that, without Our Lord, we're incomplete and life loses its purpose and meaning.

My spiritual director from many years ago used to tell me that God can do anything He wants with me if I let Him. Since in authentic love, the lover never forces himself on the beloved, God's love, expressed in grace, is never imposed upon us but instead is offered as a free invitation. He extends His hand to us, but it's up to us to grasp it. As Christians, we're called to surrender and suffer the presence of Christ in the moment. While grace may not necessarily make this easy, it will always make it possible. In doing so, we begin to see ourselves more clearly for who we are and the key role we personally play in our own struggle.

Surrender, which is far more a lifelong process than any single event, begins with a fundamental recognition that He's God and we're not. Here, we're not so much giving God something that's exclusively ours, but rather we're giving Him that which is rightfully His, our very selves. By doing so, we're not returning the gift we've received unchanged but, by faithfully living out our faith, offering our own unique gift to Him in return. This is nothing less than an act of sincere gratitude.

Catholic Tradition has long recognized grace as a remedy for our struggles, along with our need to continually surrender. This is particularly evident in the Sacrament of Reconciliation. There, we don't just ask for the forgiveness of sins as though they are external from us, but instead we say, "Bless me Father, for I have sinned." The "me" in this request is a recognition of that which is so obvious that it's often overlooked. The struggle in the interior life is first and foremost a struggle within us and by us. Consequently, it's not so much the Unholy Trinity that ensnares us, but it's we who allow the Unholy Trinity to trap us. We're the author of our own sins and, because the interior struggle arises out of a resistance to grace, we're the author of our own struggles. True, some struggles come as a result of our fallen nature, or the sins of others forced upon us, but these too can be addressed by grace. We don't author these in the same sense and, because of this, we're not always responsible for them before God. Still, to the extent grace is offered to oppose these struggles, and to the extent that we resist that grace, we're responsible for the difference. Recognizing and acknowledging this fundamental truth of the interior life allows us to take hold of it in a healthy way. It enables us to seek the necessary spiritual remedies and thereby grow in perfection.

STRUGGLE AS A WAY OF PERFECTION

> *O my Lord, inflame my heart with love for You, that my spirit may not grow weary amidst the storms, the sufferings and the trials. You see how weak I am. Love can do all.*
> **Saint Faustina, *Diary of Maria Faustina Kowalska: Divine Mercy in My Soul***

To those unfamiliar with the spiritual and mystical traditions, struggles may seem antithetical to growth in holiness. After all, aren't those who have grown in perfection more at peace within themselves? While it's certainly true that the interior life can provide a certain peace, properly understood, this peace doesn't mean the absence of struggle, at least not this side of heaven.

While we're on earth, regardless of our spiritual state, we will, to a greater or lesser degree, struggle. This is nothing less than the lifelong battle between love-of-God and love-of-self, as a result of original sin and our own personal sins. We can no more omit this struggle as it relates to our salvation than the cross could be omitted from the resurrection. Indeed, just as it was precisely in and through the cross that Jesus rose from the dead, opening up to us the gates of eternal life, so too it's precisely in and through our struggles that we will experience the fruit of Christ's redemption. This isn't at all to suggest that our struggles merit salvation. Regardless of what we do, no matter how great, no matter how noble, we're radically incapable of saving ourselves. This attitude, which is a form of Pelagianism, has been consistently condemned by the Church as heretical. It's only by responding to the grace merited to us by Jesus' own struggle, His passion and death, that we're rendered capable of uniting our struggles with His and, in that respect, work out our salvations with fear and trembling (Phil 2:12).

The saints throughout the whole of the Catholic spiritual and mystical tradition have borne witness to this "working out." When we read the unvarnished lives of the saints, we discover that it was precisely this struggle, often described as a kind of spiritual dryness, that marked much of their entire lives. Indeed, the whole canon of saints is replete with men and women who, in the pursuit of spiritual perfection, struggled. While many were well-known, such as St. Francis of Assisi, St. Anthony Claret, St. Teresa of Ávila, and St. John of the Cross, many were lesser known, such as St. Josepha Rossello, Saint Hilarion, St. Mary Magdalene de Pazzi, and St. Louise de Marillac. Perhaps one of the best-known struggles today is that of St. Thérèse of Lisieux. In her autobiography titled *The Story of a Soul*, she writes:

> I must tell you about my retreat for [religious] profession. Far from experiencing any consolation, complete aridity — desolation, almost — was my lot. Jesus was asleep in my little boat as usual. How rarely souls let Him sleep peacefully within them. Their agitation and all their requests have so tired out the Good Master that He is only too glad to enjoy the rest I offer Him. I do not suppose He will wake up until my eternal retreat, but instead of making me sad, it makes me very happy. Such an attitude of mind proves that I am far from being a saint. I should not rejoice in my aridity, but rather consider it as the result of lack of fervor and fidelity, while the fact that I often fall asleep during meditation or while making my thanksgiving should appall me. Well, I am not appalled; I bear in mind that little children are just as pleasing to their parents asleep as awake, that doctors put their patients to sleep while they perform operations, and that after all, "the Lord knows our frame. He remembers that we are but dust."[9]

In his famous *Spiritual Exercises*, St. Ignatius of Loyola spoke of this struggle in terms of consolation and desolation. Consolation arises when prayer is tranquil, blissful, and satisfying. This may happen either as a reward for our fidelity, or as a gratuitous gift from God. Similarly, desolation in prayer often comes as a means to purify us from our attachments. If we allow it, desolation can strengthen us by reminding us of our utter dependence on the grace of God. This "reminder" is a great gift, though at times in the midst of particularly intense struggles, it may seem more like a curse. Nowhere is this more beautifully illustrated than by Saint Paul in his Second Letter to the Corinthians. There, he speaks of his personal struggle as a "thorn in his flesh." He writes:

> Three times I begged the Lord about this, that it might leave me, but he said to me, "My grace is sufficient for you, for power is made perfect in weakness." I will rather boast most gladly of my weaknesses, in order that the power of Christ may dwell with me. Therefore, I am content with weaknesses, insults, hardships, persecutions, and constraints, for the sake of Christ; for when I am weak, then I am strong. (12:8–10)

Whereas consolation inspires us to persevere in prayer and devotion, desolation refines us in the fire and allows the greatest progress in the spiritual life. Anyone can pray, fulfill our obligations, and serve others when it's easy. What sacrifice is there in that? However, when we pray, fulfill our obligations, and serve others in the midst of desolation, we demonstrate our willingness to "die" for Christ. This death-to-self is nothing less than an expression of love, an act of gratitude in response to the great gifts we've already received. St. Pio of Pietrelcina often observed that the life of a Christian is nothing but a perpetual struggle against self. There is, he taught, no flowering of the soul except at the price of pain.

When accomplished in desolation, our prayers, the fulfilment of our obligations, and indeed our Christian service, are far more powerful than those very same acts done in consolation. As St. John Eudes reminds us, "You can advance farther in grace in one hour during this time of affliction than in many days during a time of consolation." Similarly, St. Francis de Sales writes:

> Our actions are like roses, which when fresh have more beauty but when dry have more strength and sweetness. In like manner, our works performed with tenderness of heart are more agreeable to ourselves I say, who regard only our own satisfaction. Yet when performed in times of dryness, they possess more sweetness and become more precious in the sight of God.[10]

Desolation provides us with unique opportunities to source our love in Christ the Servant by uniting our struggles in union with His timeless eternal sacrifice. These become, if we see them in faith, grace-filled moments enabling us to live out our vocations in fidelity to the will of God. They provide occasions to "offer-up" our imperfect sacrifices and, through Him, make them perfect, transforming us in the very process. All of this, when done in a state of grace, leads to greater intimacy with Our Lord.

Understood this way, struggle does not mark a failure in the spiritual life but a vitality. Struggle is our effort, united with and inspired by grace, to overcome our sinful ways and seek, imperfectly as it may be, a life of virtue and sanctity. Struggle, therefore, deserves a place at the beginning of any consideration of Catholic spirituality. This is particularly true for those new to the interior life, as it often begins with a "honeymoon" period, inevitably followed by a dive into the spiritual abyss. As St. Philip Neri counsels, "As a rule, people who aim at a spiritual life begin with the sweet and afterward pass on to the bitter. So now, away with all tepidity, off with that mask of yours, carry your cross, don't leave it to carry you."[11]

While struggle in the interior life has its place, we should neither deliberately seek it nor merely tolerate it when it could be remedied. This is not to deny its redemptive value, but we have equal responsibility to diminish our struggles when possible so that what remains can be taken up in the interior life. God never gives us more than we can handle, but sometimes we do. If, for example, we're struggling in prayer because we're in a noisy place, then instead of offering it up, we should move. That's our first obligation. If we're unable to move, then by all means we should offer it up. All too often we tend to impose a pseudo-cross upon ourselves. This can occur for many reasons, sometimes because of scrupulosity and other times because this pseudo-cross diverts us from our real cross. To use the previous example, when the actual reason we're praying in a noisy place is because we'd rather not face God in the silence of our hearts, then prayer becomes an avoidance rather that an encounter.

For those spiritual struggles we can't avoid, the best remedy is perseverance. This is nothing less than an act of fidelity to the God who created us out of love and saved us while we were still sinners. In its most basic sense, perseverance is tenacity in the interior life despite the difficulties. It's the persistence necessary, this side of heaven, to work through the challenges that impede us from intimate communion with Christ the Servant. In this regard, perseverance doesn't simply consist of passively enduring our struggles, much the same way we might hunker down in the midst of a terrible storm. Instead, perseverance consists of actively engaging in the struggle by applying a spiritual remedy so that the very struggle becomes a means of holiness. Fortunately, we have a rich inheritance left to us by the saints and mystics of the Church who fought these very same battles and, with grace, won. As a result, there is much we can learn from them. In his book *Christ Is Passing By*, St. Josemaría Escrivá observes:

> A Christian's struggle must be unceasing, for interior life consists in beginning and beginning again. This prevents us from proudly thinking that we are perfect already. It is inevitable that we should meet difficulties on our way. If we did not come up against obstacles, we would not be creatures of flesh and blood. We will always have passions which pull us downwards; we will always have to defend ourselves against more or less self-defeating urges.[12]

Beyond the call for divine help, which should be constant, what else can we do in the midst of interior struggle? If we're struggling with dryness in the spiritual life, St. Jane Frances de Chantal assures us that, "The great method of prayer is to have none. If, in going to prayer, one can form in oneself a pure capacity for receiving the Spirit of God, that will suffice for all method."[13] This wise advice speaks not to the prayer itself but to our interior disposition while praying. It reminds us that, at its most fundamental level, prayer isn't a question of "what" but "whom." It guides us from the thing being done to the One to whom our prayers are directed. This is made possible when we adopt an inner attitude of receptivity, despite the often-frenetic pace of our lives. It requires us, to the extent possible, to slow down and take a breath before prayer. It obliges us to calm ourselves, preparing not so much to speak to God but to hear him, not so much to do something but to be with Him.

Notice here that prayer, and indeed all spiritual works, are not ends in themselves. We don't pray for prayer's sake any more than we converse for conversation's sake. Like conversation, prayer mediates and allows for an encounter with the other, the absence of which robs the encounter of its very purpose, interpersonal communion. It's all too easy to lose sight of this and, feeling our prayers as useless, to stop praying. Here, St. Alphonsus Liguori's counsel is particularly helpful:

> This, then, is your answer whenever you feel tempted to stop praying because it seems to be a waste of time: "I am here to please God." The measure of prayer isn't whether it pleases us, but whether it pleases God; and our willingness to persevere for His glory will, in turn, aid our own spiritual growth.[14]

Because we're body-soul composites, good spiritual advice should always be accompanied by equally good practical advice. When we struggle, it's often helpful to keep our prayers short and simple. After all, God already knows the complexities of our hearts better than we do. We don't need to convince Him of our concerns with compelling arguments; we only need appeal to Him from the depths of our hearts with sincerity. When his spiritual directees were dry as dust in prayer, St. Paul of the Cross counseled them not to quit and to keep going using short prayers.

Struggles in the interior life, particularly when they're experienced as a dryness, can also be dealt with effectively through Eucharistic adoration. In prayer, as noted earlier, we needn't have the words but simply the willingness to sit quietly with Our Lord. Silence, especially before the Blessed Sacrament, can have a consoling effect, especially when it's focused on the Real Presence. Simply acknowledging Jesus fully present, Body, Blood, Soul, and Divinity, has a grace in itself and is well worth the effort. In a similar sense, realize that when we pray, we always do so in the presence of our guardian angel. Of this, St. John Vianney reminds us that, "If you find it impossible to pray, hide behind your good angel, and charge him to pray in your stead."[15]

MEDITATIONS AND REFLECTIONS
As discussed earlier, this final section is designed to allow a deeper, more personal absorption of the material just covered. It consists of a set of two interrelated spiritual exercises whose sole purpose is to reengage the key themes in this chapter so as to internalize the truths they contain. This approach is based on the fundamental conviction that by prayerfully reflecting and meditating on these truths, you allow God to speak to you in a way that will draw you into a deeper, more intimate communion with Christ the Servant. Each exercise should begin with at least a minute or two of relaxed silence, disposing your heart to the encounter. This should be followed by either a short extemporaneous prayer or, if you choose, the following:

> *Heavenly Father, I open my heart up to You so that, through the power of Your most Holy Spirit, I may encounter Your Son, Christ the Servant, in a deeply personal and transformative way. Forgive my sins and free me from the attachments of this world so that I am better attentive to Your presence and, in this attentiveness, hear what You want me to hear. Give me the grace to abandon myself to You in this moment for, in the depths of my soul, I want nothing more than You. Speak Lord, Your servant listens. Mary, Mother of Christ the Servant, pray for me. Amen.*

KEY THEMES
The following represent some key themes found in this chapter. As you reflect on them, consider what Christ the Servant is revealing about Himself and, more importantly, what He's reveal-

ing about you. In this you're asking two distinct but related questions: Lord, what are You saying *in general* and, flowing from this, what are You saying specifically *to me*. Ponder how what is said may impact your relationship to Him, and how this may influence your relationship with others, particularly in the choices you make. Remember, as you meditate upon these things, to write down your thoughts in your journal or spiritual notebook. This may be a single word, a sentence, a paragraph, or even more. The purpose here is to capture the most important elements of your meditation, even if they are not whole or complete.

Recall that what is offered in these exercises is by way of a pious recommendation. You are free to fully engage or completely omit them as you see fit. Should you decide to move forward, you may take on one, some, or even all of the themes as the Spirit prompts you. This exercise, and its effectiveness, rely on grace and your openness to that grace. With all of this in mind, the key themes are as follows:

- Primacy of the spiritual life
- The interior life as a place of encounter
- The distinctiveness of servant spirituality
- The importance of empathy
- Struggle in the spiritual life
- Surrender as abandonment

REFLECTION QUESTIONS

Now that you have meditated upon these themes and captured what Christ the Servant may be saying to you, you can explore them further in the following six reflection questions. It's recommended that this be done in a separate sitting, giving you a chance to digest the fruit of your meditation. If you do choose to turn to the reflection questions in a separate sitting, begin again with silence and prayer as described above. As with the key themes, write down your insights and thoughts in your journal or spiritual notebook.

- Identify two or three things you learned from this chapter that you didn't know before.
- Identify two or three key insights you gained through this chapter into your spiritual life, family, God, or the Church.
- Identify two or three ideas to apply your learning and insights from this chapter to your life as a Catholic.
- How might reading this chapter and reflecting on the key themes found within it deepen your *relationship to Christ the Servant*?
- How might reading this chapter and reflecting on the key themes found within it deepen your *identity in Christ the Servant*?
- How might reading this chapter and reflecting on the key themes found within it deepen your *mission with Christ the Servant*?

Chapter Three
The Necessity of Surrender

Imagine that this Lord Himself is at your side and see how lovingly and how humbly He is teaching you — and, believe me, you should stay with so good a Friend for as long as you can before you leave Him. If you become accustomed to having Him at your side, and if He sees that you love Him to be there and are always trying to please Him, you will never be able to send Him away, nor will He ever fail you. He will help you in all your trials and you will have Him everywhere. Do you think it's a small thing to have such a Friend as that beside you?
St. Teresa of Ávila, *The Way of Perfection*

Divine abandonment means surrendering our lives to God's will. The term *surrender*, as it relates to abandonment, is quite instructive. In its broadest sense, it means to stop fighting.

Surrender presupposes and reveals the interior battle we all experience as a result of our fallen yet redeemed nature. Though Baptism freed us from original sin and incorporated us into the Church, concupiscence — that is, the tendency to sin — remains. To abandon ourselves to the divine will is to diminish the battle within us, the battle between selflessness and selfishness, the battle between virtue and vice, the battle between good and evil. Of course, this battle will not end until we draw our last breath. Still, by abandoning ourselves to the will of God we can, with grace, not only survive this battle, but triumph.

Surrender isn't so much an event as a lifelong process often characterized by an interior conflict. Like struggle, far from being a sign of failure, inner conflict is a hallmark of the spiritual life. Applied to abandonment, it typically occurs in two stages paralleling the two powers of the soul, the intellect and the will. The intellect perceives a truth and the need to correspond to it by changing our way of life. Here, in the exercise of our conscience, we know something is wrong and realize that to be right with God and at peace within ourselves, we need to reform. The desire to reform is only the first stage of the battle. It's a kind of spiritual awakening on the intellectual level, a perception of the difference between what's good and how we haven't lived up to it. Though this intellectual conflict is good because it admits our need to move beyond where we are to a better place with God, by itself it's not enough. To advance toward divine abandonment, we must take up the second stage, that of the will. Whereas the intellect seeks the truth, the will seeks the good. It's associated with specific concrete acts. So, for example, in order to be faithful to what we believe, we must maintain custody of the tongue. Gossip among all Christians is always wrong. When we gossip, especially when it becomes calumny (CCC 2479), we sin, and when we sin, we weaken our relationship with God. Our intellects grasp this truth, and our consciences are formed by it. However, if our understanding is limited merely to this intellectual stage, and never incorporated into our will and actions — such that we persist in doing evil — it will eat us from the inside out. Alignment between the intellect and the will, how we think and how we choose, as these are shaped by God's Revelation regarding how we are to grow in grace and perfection in Him, allows us to experience a kind of integrity and, as a direct result, live in bold confidence.

Of course, the movement between the intellect and the will requires considerable work characterized by stops and starts. This is precisely why it's often described as a battle. By ourselves, this movement is almost impossible, but with grace, all things are possible. Grace, God's supernatural help, enables us to move our interior conflicts, perhaps ever-so-slowly at first, from the intellect to the will. It allows us to participate with Him such that we cooperate in our own salvation (Phil 2:12) and, through our life and ministry, in the salvation of others. In this sense, interior conflict becomes the "place" of purification and sanctification. It's nothing less than our cross leading to our resurrection. Despite the ongoing frustrations associated with this conflict, it's part and parcel of the surrender necessary to abandon ourselves to the divine will.

Properly understood, surrender is grounded in a response to a divine love already received. When we grow in awareness of how much God loves us, we're overwhelmed with joy and, in gratitude, want to respond to Him in kind. This means allowing His will to shape and direct our desires and plans. In this respect, we never lose our will, we never become mere automatons in the hands of God, but instead permit His revelation of a personal love in Christ to purify and perfect our wills. As a result, our wills, indeed our entire lives, become what they should be and in this slow and sometimes arduous process, we paradoxically discover who we really are, and what we're really called to do.

As both the Scriptures and Tradition attest, there's no way to cultivate the interior life and grow in intimate communion without some form of divine abandonment. We need only recall the lives of Abraham, Moses, Job, and the prophets in the Old Testament. Likewise, in the New Testament, we remember the Blessed Virgin Mary, John the Baptist, Peter, and the other apostles. Of course, the greatest example of abandonment is Jesus Christ. His entire life, death, and resurrection was nothing less than a perfect example of surrender to the Father's will. Indeed, He was quite explicit about this when He said to His apostles, "I came down from heaven not to do my own will but the will of the one who sent me" (Jn 6:38).

His abandonment didn't waiver, despite the trial that would ensue. During the agony in the garden of Gethsemane, Jesus prayed, "Father, if you are willing, take this cup away from me; still, not my will but yours be done" (Lk 22:42). Jesus' words, and His subsequent passion, reveal that abandonment to the divine will carries with it a personal hardship. Consider the trials of Job (Job 1:11), or the sword that pierced Mary's heart (Lk 2:35), or the prediction of Peter's martyrdom (Jn 21:18–19). Jesus Himself knew well of this conflict as He spread His arms on the cross for us. All of these examples illustrate that there's a real cost associated with abandonment, for it's in its most fundamental sense nothing less than a response to Jesus' invitation, "Whoever wishes to come after me must deny himself, take up his cross, and follow me" (Mt 16:24). Abandonment, properly understood, is not a purely human effort to follow Jesus but rather a grace-filled response to a God who has already drawn close to us.

Like the Scriptures, Tradition is replete with saints and mystics abandoning themselves to the divine will amid great struggles. Certainly, one of the most noteworthy is St. Augustine of Hippo. His was a long and arduous process, which he describes in book eight of his *Confessions*. At a critical point in his conversion, he admits to himself that "I had now found the priceless pearl and I ought to have sold all that I had and bought it — yet I hesitated."[1] In this, the great saint reveals an internal battle of two wills — one pulling him to divine abandonment and the other pulling him to his own sinful desires. Properly understood, these are not two distinct wills, but a figurative way of saying that his will is torn between two distinct alternatives. The conflict between these two "wills" intensifies the perception of his own sinfulness. Praying, he says to God, "And now you set me face to face with myself, that I might see how ugly I was, and how crooked and sordid, bespotted and ulcerous. And I looked and I loathed myself."[2]

In the midst of this struggle, Augustine sees, with ever-greater clarity, the impact of his sins and realizes he must repent. Still, between what he knows he must do (in his intellect), and what he must actually do — that is, choose with his will to follow his intellect — there is a great chasm. Such a movement means a radical conversion — giving up the many sins that have, up to this point, defined his life. In deep anguish and near despair, he walks with his friend Alypius into the courtyard. Augustine's struggle at this point has become so intense that Alypius, unable to console him, leaves his friend in solitude, while remaining at a distance. Shortly thereafter, Augustine falls to the ground, sobbing uncontrollably. In his anguish, and using the words of the psalmist, he cries out, "How long, O Lord?" Of this moment, Augustine later reflects, "I was saying these things and weeping in the most bitter contrition of my heart, when suddenly I heard the voice of a boy or a girl (I know not which) — coming from the neighboring house, chanting over and over again. 'Pick it up, read it; pick it up, read it.'"[3]

Returning to Alypius, Augustine takes up the Scriptures and randomly opens them to Saint Paul's Letter to the Romans. There he reads, "[L]et us conduct ourselves properly as in the day, not in orgies and drunkenness, not in promiscuity and licentiousness, not in rivalry and jealousy" (Rom 13:13). These very sins described his struggle with uncanny accuracy. Later he would say of this moment, "I wanted to read no further, nor did I need to. For instantly, as the sentence ended, there was infused in my heart something like the light of full certainty and all the gloom of doubt vanished away."[4]

AWARENESS OF THE EVER-PRESENT GOD

> *God is everywhere ... and the fullness of His majesty is present even in hidden and secret places.*
> **St. Cyprian of Carthage, *Treatise on the Lord's Prayer***

The work of the eighteenth-century French Jesuit, Jean-Pierre de Caussade, provides a starting point for our consideration of abandonment as it applies to servant spirituality. Because it speaks of surrender to God as its core element, it illustrates an essential first step in all spiritualities. This step establishes the boundaries in the relationship with an indispensable twofold truth; namely, God is God, and we're not. This recognition, which is far more a lifetime coming-to-know than a single insight, gives rise to the realization that without union with Him, we're incomplete, and our lives lack true meaning and purpose. As St. Thomas Aquinas writes, "the will's desire is satisfied by the divine good alone as its last end."[5] Put another way, only God can satisfy our deepest longing and, in doing so, enable us to live in eternal happiness.

Surrender to God represents the first step to union with Him, for it's nothing less than an act of love. It represents an abandonment of the will that, paradoxically, enables us to more fully appropriate and refine it. This truth enabled Saint Augustine to boldly proclaim, "Love God and do what you will."[6] Augustine understood well that if we truly love God, if we abandon our will to His, our entire lives will be transformed. This bond of love means that His desires become our desires, His choices become our choices, and His mission becomes our mission. Here we don't lose our identity, but instead discover it, becoming more fully who we are. Divine love, when accepted and internalized, makes possible an incarnation of sorts, enabling us, as Christians, to bear witness to Christ the Servant.

Jean-Pierre de Caussade was born in Southern France in 1675, more than a century after the Protestant Reformation. It was the time of the Catholic Counter-Reformation, which brought with it not only the establishment of the seminary system and the reform of clerical life but a spiritual revival. Preceding de Caussade were such towering figures as Philip Neri, Francis de Sales, Jane Frances de Chantal, Ignatius of Loyola, Teresa of Ávila, and John of the Cross. Notable in this movement was a growing understanding that holiness is not limited to priestly and religious life, but includes the lay faithful as well. While this would come to fruition in the Second Vatican Council's universal call to holiness, it nonetheless had its roots in the spiritual approaches of the sixteenth and seventeenth centuries, of which de Caussade would have been a beneficiary. He writes:

> Therefore, do I preach abandonment, and not any particular state. Every state in which souls are placed by Your grace is the same to me. I teach a general method by which all can attain the state which You have marked out for them. I do not exact more than the will to abandon themselves to Your guidance. You will make them arrive infallibly at the state which is best for them. It's faith that I preach; abandonment, confidence, and faith; the will to be subject to, and to be the tool of the divine action, and to believe that at every moment this action

is working in every circumstance, provided that the soul has more or less good-will.[7]

We know relatively little of de Caussade's life. At the age of eighteen, he entered the Society of Jesus. Ordained to the priesthood in 1704, he was later sent to Toulouse where he obtained a doctorate in theology. De Caussade became proficient in Greek, Latin, philosophy, and physics. Some years later, he became the spiritual director to the Visitation Sisters in Nancy. Spiritual writings ascribed to de Caussade were first published after his death by fellow Jesuit Henri Ramière in 1861 under the title *L'Abandon à la Providence Divine*, better known today by its English title *Abandonment to Divine Providence*. The work is said to be a compilation of letters sent to the sisters in his absence. While recent scholarship has questioned de Caussade's authorship, this in no way undermines the work's great value as a spiritual classic.

It should be noted that, in taking up de Caussade's work as an important dimension to a servant spirituality, it will not be presented as a kind of exposition or a full synopsis. It will, instead, act as an inspiration and guide. Although there are a great many universals found in his thought, he was writing in a particular time to a particular audience. In this respect, a number of nuances proper to eighteenth-century Catholicism will not apply to us today, at least not directly. What I hope to do here instead is to take these universals and apply them to servant spirituality as it exists today. In this respect, should the reader wish a more complete presentation of the *Abandonment to Divine Providence*, he should read the work in its entirety.

De Caussade echoes much of the spiritual tradition of his time by acknowledging that God continues to reveal Himself — though, unlike the public revelations in the apostolic age that belong to the Sacred Deposit of Faith, such revelations of which de Caussade speaks are directed to individuals.[8] These personal revelations deepen and enrich what God has already revealed in the Church's foundation, much the same way spousal love is deepened and enriched over time. As the years progress, spouses don't discover someone new, but through the triumphs and tragedies of life, they grow in a deeper understanding and appreciation of the other. In a similar manner, personal revelations unfold what God has already revealed, but they do so in a particular moment, to an individual. They are meant to touch, in concrete terms, the person in his or her life, as he or she lives out the Faith. This unfolding allows the Faith to be personally appropriated and integrated into the life of the believer. Put more figuratively, it allows the Faith to move between the head and the heart. I say "between" the head and heart because, properly understood, the head and heart set up a dialectic of sorts, a kind of back-and-forth, in which the Faith is understood (head), and then personally appropriated (heart). Once appropriated, the heart desires more, because love desires more, and so it seeks to understand more.

All of this is predicated on the understanding that God's Revelation is not merely a sharing of His plan of salvation, but a sharing of His very self. More to the point, it's an offer of divine love, and we simply cannot love what we don't understand. This means the whole person, head and heart, come together in saying "yes" to the offer of divine love. Personal revelation finds its authenticity and legitimacy when it is consistent with Divine Revelation as expressed in the Sacred Scriptures and interpreted by the Church. Depending on the gravity of such revelations, they may need to be discussed with a spiritual director, confessor, spouse, or even trusted confidant. This is because, as Saint John warns, "Beloved, do not trust every spirit but test the spirits to see whether they belong to God, because many false prophets have gone out into the world" (1 Jn 4:1).

GOD'S HIDDEN OPERATIONS

> *Where can I go from your spirit?*
> *From your presence, where can I flee?*
> *If I ascend to the heavens, you are there;*
> *if I lie down in Sheol, there you are.*
> **Psalm 139:7-8**

De Caussade speaks of these revelations as God's "hidden operations." Embedded in the very fabric of our lives, in the people we meet, in the situations we encounter, God speaks to us. To say that "God speaks" isn't to suggest a literal voice from heaven. Though this is certainly not beyond His power, divine locutions are not His typical mode of communication. Instead, God speaks to the soul with a voice that only the soul can hear. This "Divine Voice" arises not so much in silence itself but in the silence that follows prayerful meditation and reflection on the events of our lives. These events are not limited to major turning points but, more often than not, in the simple comings and goings of our day that — and this is important — give rise to certain duties. This said, and before we get ahead of ourselves, it will be necessary to consider how the Church understands the presence of God.

The Church has long taught that, like omniscience (all knowing) and omnipotence (all powerful), omnipresence (ever present) is one of the divine attributes. Put another way, this means that God is everywhere, such that there is no aspect of reality apart from His presence. In this respect, God is not contained in the world, but the world is contained in God. St. Thomas Aquinas spoke of it this way: "God is in all things by His power, inasmuch as all things are subject to His power; He is by His presence in all things, inasmuch as all things are bare and open to His eyes; He is in all things by His essence, inasmuch as He is present to all as the cause of their being."⁹

This means that God infuses and penetrates every aspect of reality. In his famous Breastplate, Saint Patrick spoke of it this way, "Christ beside me, Christ before me, Christ behind me, Christ within me, Christ beneath me, Christ above me." While we may apprehend His presence in varying degrees depending on the situation, this limitation is only on our part since God has no such limitation. Simply put, "God is." Thus, while we can, figuratively speaking, turn our backs on Him, He is nonetheless always present to us. To better appreciate God's presence as it relates to divine abandonment and servant spirituality, it will be helpful to consider the manner in which God revealed Himself in the Book of Exodus.

While tending the flock of his father-in-law, Jethro, at the foot of Mount Horeb, Moses encountered an angel in the form of a bush that, while on fire, was not consumed. After a brief dialog with God, from which he would be sent on a mission, Moses asked: "If I go to the Israelites and say to them, 'The God of your ancestors has sent me to you,' and they ask me, 'What is his name?' what do I tell them? God replied to Moses: I am who I am. Then he added: This is what you will tell the Israelites: I AM has sent me to you" (Ex 3:13–14).

In Greek and Roman mythology, when the gods came to earth, they typically did so in a violent and competitive fashion. Something in this world had to diminish or be destroyed in order for them to make themselves present. The realm of the gods and the realm of men were mutually exclusive, never the twain should meet. Consequently, in these great sagas, when men stood in the physical presence of the gods, they were often weakened or even killed. This was not the case with the God of Israel. When God draws near to Moses, His presence (exhibited in the fire) does not consume the bush (which reflects us). Both the material and the spiritual worlds coexist side-by-side. In this respect, God's presence does not destroy us. He doesn't compete violently with us. Instead, He illuminates us, radiating His glory in every direction. When we open ourselves up to the presence of God already within us, we become more fully alive, more perfect, more beautiful. As a result, we then become a source of light for others.

After Moses is given his mission, he asks for God's name. To this he receives the reply, "I am who I am." Keep in mind, Moses was raised an Egyptian prince and, after escaping pharaoh, was living in the Sinai Peninsula among nomadic tribes. Both the Egyptians and these tribes worshiped many gods. From this perspective, Moses was asking a rather commonsensical question: "When the Israelites ask me your name, what do I tell them?" Moses, in a desire to better fulfill his mission, seeks to ground that mission in the one who sends him. As a result, he wants to distinguish this deity from all others. But God doesn't answer Moses' question, at least not directly. He simply says, "I am who I am ... tell the Israelites: I AM has sent me to you."

The Catholic Tradition has found this passage deeply theological, concealing as much as it reveals. In His response to Moses, God isn't implying that He's just a type of being, nor is He suggesting that He's one being among many. He's not even indicating that He's the greatest being ever. Rather, He is being itself. Later theologians, led by St. Thomas Aquinas, would speak of God as *ipsum esse subsistens* — that is, *being itself subsisting*. To be sure, this is a kind of "head-scratching" mystery for both theologians and non-theologians alike. Thankfully, for our purposes, we needn't plumb the depths of metaphysics. We need only observe that, for Saint Thomas and others, God doesn't fit in any single category of being.

To better appreciate what I mean here, consider that, when we want to know about something, we tend to place it in a familiar category. If, for example, I ask, "What's that in your hands?"

You might respond, "It's a book." Immediately, you've situated the unknown object in a familiar category, thus making it known, at least on a basic level. By putting things in various known categories, we can identify and differentiate them, enabling us to compare and contrast them to other things. This is the way our minds work. This is the way we come to know. However, Saint Thomas asserts that God, as He has been revealed to us, can't be put into any category, not even the category of being. He is neither "this thing," nor "that thing," nor even the biggest thing. He is the sheer act of being itself. If God were one thing among many, He would by necessity have to displace us, figuratively speaking, pushing us out of the way when we encounter Him. Just as I'm unable to move into your space without moving you, so it would be with a god who is simply another thing. That god, like the gods of Greek and Roman mythology, would have to violate our space and compete with us aggressively. But a God who is the sheer act of being can enter intimately into His creatures in a non-destructive and noncompetitive way. As the soul animates the body and gives it life, so God permeates and penetrates the lives of those who respond to His divine invitation.

Nowhere is the coexistence between the spiritual and material, between the divine and human, expressed more profoundly than in the Incarnation. According to the *Catechism*:

> The unique and altogether singular event of the Incarnation of the Son of God does not mean that Jesus Christ is part God and part man, nor does it imply that he is the result of a confused mixture of the divine and the human. He became truly man while remaining truly God. Jesus Christ is true God and true man. (464)

The Incarnation reveals that human beings were created, from the very beginning, to receive the divine more perfectly than a hand to a glove. Though, in our case, sin distorts the fit, grace restores it. If this is true, and we believe that it is, then does it not follow that we were made for God such that, in Him, we live, and move, and have our being (Acts 17:28)?

By better grasping the nature of God and our ultimate end in Him, we can begin to see how His omnipresence means that every single moment of our lives can represent a kind of personal revelation. This revelation, in turn, can represent an opportunity for prayer. As St. Paul of the Cross observed, "By habitually thinking of the presence of God, we succeed in praying twenty-four hours a day. The continual remembrance of the presence of God engenders in the soul a divine state." This isn't at all to suggest that God expects us to be so attentive to His revelation that we cease to live out our lives, stuck in a kind of perpetual listening and thereby neglecting our vocational responsibilities. Instead, it means that as we live out our lives, in the very midst of living out our vocation, God's revelation is made known to us. Here, we must take great care not to try and escape this world to find God, for if we do that, we will only succeed in passing Him on the way. He is always present, enmeshed in the very fabric of our lives.

This understanding of God is important to our consideration of abandonment because we can tend to see the spiritual life as a zero-sum gain. This is to say, the more I give to God, the less there is for me, my spouse, my children, my ministry, etc. In a zero-sum gain each participant's gain or loss is proportionate to the gains or losses of the others. Perhaps an example would prove helpful. My wife and I are blessed with many children. Over the years, as the numbers grew, well-intended people have asked, "How do you do it?" The unspoken assumption has been that the love and strength that inspires the raising of children diminishes with each child. It's certainly true that we humans are limited and, as a result, can be overwhelmed at times, but by co-operating with grace we can extend those limitations. We can be, with God, far more than we can be without Him. In this respect, love isn't a divider, but a multiplier.

By abandoning ourselves to divine providence, by slowly surrendering ourselves to the love of God, we don't lose our life. Instead, we gain it. This is precisely what Jesus meant when He spoke of discipleship, "Whoever wishes to come after me must deny himself, take up his cross, and follow me. For whoever wishes to save his life will lose it, but whoever loses his life for my sake will find it" (Mt 16:24–25). Divine abandonment means giving it all, holding nothing back, and trusting that God will provide. So, with God there's not only room for our spouses, our children, and our ministry, but the room for each of these grows within us. It's not that God miraculously expands the hours of the day and our energy in a quantitative sense. Rather, by abandoning ourselves to His love, the quality of our time with each of these is enriched and enlivened. This is because God, who is present in that moment, infuses that very moment with grace.

In the pursuit of divine abandonment, it's not unusual for some to slip into the extreme of providentialism. In its most basic sense, providentialism is the belief that all events are controlled by God. It's a form of fatalism that fails to see that the abandonment talked about by the saints and mystics requires an active engagement with God. We don't become a kind of puppet, responding to the strings God pulls. Because He loves us, ours is a participation in His divine will where we don't lose our own will but instead direct it to what is true, good, and beautiful. This is analogous to a strong sacramental marriage where the two share in one life, albeit as two distinct individuals. Thus, my will is shaped and influenced by my wife's will, while always remaining my will. Because it remains my will, the acts that flow are my acts; the love that's given is my love.

THE SACRAMENT OF THE PRESENT MOMENT

> *The events of every moment bear the impress of the will of God, and of His adorable Name. How holy is this name! It's right, therefore, to bless it, to treat it as a kind of sacrament which by its own virtue sanctifies those souls which place no obstacles in its way.*
> **Jean-Pierre de Caussade, *Abandonment to Divine Providence***

Thus far, we've examined the primacy of the interior life, the distinctiveness of servant spirituality, and divine abandonment as these relate to the ever-present God. To appreciate these foundational points as they pertain to the life and ministry of the laity, we now turn to what de Caussade calls "the sacrament of the present moment," or more often "the present moment." The present moment is the realization that the ever-present God makes Himself known to us through everyday events such as the people we meet, the places we go, and even in our struggles. Of this de Caussade writes, "God continues to speak today as He spoke in former times to our fathers when there were no [spiritual] directors as at present, nor any regular method of direction."[10]

The "speech of God" is a figurative way of describing how God communicates with us. This is also known as Divine Revelation. By Divine Revelation, the Church means God's self-disclosure of who He is and His plan for our salvation. There are three kinds of revelation, the most important of which is public. The Fathers of the Second Vatican Council in the Dogmatic Constitution on Divine Revelation described public Revelation this way:

> After God had spoken many times and in various ways through the prophets, "in these last days He has spoken

to us by a Son." For He sent His Son, the eternal Word who enlightens all men, to dwell among men and to tell them about the inner life of God. Hence, Jesus Christ, sent as "a man among men" ... accomplishes the saving work which the Father gave Him to do. As a result, He Himself ... completed and perfected Revelation and confirmed it with divine guarantees ... no new public revelation is to be expected before the glorious manifestation of our Lord, Jesus Christ.[11]

Public Revelation, found in Scripture and Tradition, constitutes the sacred Deposit of Faith, that which all believers are called to believe. While it's complete in the sense that mankind has received all that is needed for salvation, it hasn't been made completely explicit. Consequently, "it remains for Christian faith gradually to grasp its full significance over the course of the centuries" (CCC 66). As the authentic guardian of the Faith, the Magisterium, or teaching office of the Church — that is, the bishops in union with the pope — under the guidance of the Holy Spirit, interpret this Revelation, keeping it free from error. Because of this, the faithful, precisely because they have chosen to be faithful, are to accept these revealed truths with a divine faith. To explicitly reject revealed truths such as the Incarnation, the Real Presence, or even the existence of Satan, would constitute an infidelity.

Unlike public Revelation, which ended with the death of the last apostle, private revelation is meant to emphasize that which has already been revealed. It's a divine message, given through a certain person or persons, that enables the faithful to grow in holiness. According to the *Catechism*, "Throughout the ages, there have been so-called 'private' revelations, some of which have been recognized by the authority of the Church. ... It is not their role to improve or complete Christ's definitive Revelation, but to help live more fully by it" (67). Those who have received private revelation include many saints, such as St. Catherine of Siena, St. Teresa of Ávila, St. John of the Cross, St. Margaret Mary Alacoque, and St. Faustina Kowalska, to name a few. Private revelation also includes the various apparitions of the Blessed Virgin Mary as she speaks on behalf of her Son. Some of the more well-known are Guadalupe, Rue du Bac, La Salette, Lourdes, and Fatima. The authenticity of any private revelation, be it purportedly from the saints or the Blessed Mother, lies in its agreement with public revelation. Although the Church may officially recognize and approve the content of these private revelations, they neither belong to, nor add anything to, the sacred Deposit of Faith. They simply emphasize that which has already been revealed, inspiring the faithful to grow in deeper communion with God. As a result, the faithful are not required to accept private revelation. That said, for anyone wishing to grow in holiness, it would be imprudent not to at least investigate the implications of private revelation to the interior life.

Personal revelation is another kind of revelation that God gives to an individual to discern His will in a particular situation. Like private revelation, personal revelation requires for its authenticity agreement with public Revelation and the teachings of the Church. It can express itself in such things as discerning a vocation, a new job, a move, or even a major expense. Personal revelation is based on two fundamental truths. First, that God loves us and cares about every detail of our lives. Because of this, He provides to all who are open to it the interior insights necessary to live the Christian life. For those seeking a servant spirituality, this would include a deep and constant revelation of Christ the Servant as He relates to our identity and mission. The second fundamental truth is that we possess reason and free will, and God wants us to use these to do good and avoid evil. Where the first truth concerns the interior life, the second pertains to the exterior life.

The sacrament of the present moment represents a kind of personal revelation that is constant and ongoing. Unlike other kinds of personal revelation, it doesn't concern itself with some specific thing such as a vocation, job, or house, but instead focuses on an ongoing awareness of God's presence in the hereand now. As de Caussade points out, "What treasures of grace lie concealed in these moments filled, apparently, by the most ordinary events. That which is visible might happen to anyone, but the invisible, discerned by faith, is no less than God operating very great things."[12] The present moment provides, if we have the eyes to see, divine encounters that reveal something of God.

While de Caussade treats this personal revelation broadly, such that every moment reveals the majesty of God, for our purposes we will assume this approach and build upon it. In other words, we will advance de Caussade's thought by considering its application to servant spirituality. Here, our concern is how the sacrament of the present moment allows us to see the suffering Christ in the needs of others and to respond to those needs effectively. Before doing so however, some important distinctions are in order.

As noted earlier, servant spirituality is a lay form of diaconal spirituality. Therefore, it's from the diaconate that lay servant spirituality draws its inspiration and example. Because of his ordination to the diaconate, the deacon has been configured, on the deepest level of his being, to Christ the Servant. As such, he's the sacred custodian of ecclesial service, bearing witness to Christ the Servant by "incarnating" Him in the life of the Church. In this respect, he's called, as revealed in the groundbreaking work of John N. Collins, to be an ambassador or emissary.[13] This understanding of the diaconate, and its implication to servant spirituality, will be taken up in the next chapter. That said, it's sufficient to note that a brief consideration of the deacon's approach to the sacrament of the present moment will prove helpful for understanding a lay spirituality of service.

It's this role of being an ambassador or emissary, arising from his diaconal ordination, that reorients the deacon as he approaches the sacrament of the present moment. Consequently, the deacon, while attentive to all that God wants to reveal to him, must be particularly attentive to the needs of others and how these needs might be fulfilled. For the servant, in this case the deacon, to serve the master, he must know what the master needs and when he needs it. Simply put, the servant must love the master through specific concrete acts. This side of heaven, we can't love God directly any more than we can serve Him directly. We can, however, love and serve Him through others. Recall the words of Jesus in Matthew's Gospel, "Amen, I say to you, whatever you did for one of these least brothers of mine, you did for me" (Mt 25:40). Because the deacon is called to reveal Christ the Servant in a preeminent way, he is an example for the laity, particularly those who are called to holiness through a servant spirituality.

When de Caussade wrote to the sisters in the eighteenth century, the term *duty* within the spiritual tradition was understood as an obligation arising out of a divine love already bestowed. It's a concrete application of the virtue of religion, which itself is an expression of the cardinal virtue of justice. Here, duty is understood as rendering to God what is due. It's repaying a debt we can never really repay but which was repaid on our behalf through the redemptive love of Christ on the cross. As St. Ambrose of Milan observes, "The rich man who gives to the poor does not bestow alms but pays a debt." We are "rich" because we have received God's mercy. It's only when this debt is united with Christ's own love, and offered back to the Father, that our duty has been fulfilled. It's Christ and Christ alone who makes up our deficit and, in doing so, bridges the gap between what was given and what is returned, thereby satisfying our duty. This isn't a one-time event but, because God continues to pour out His love upon us, a constant and ongoing reality, a kind of reciprocity that never ends unless we end it. De Caussade describes duty this way:

> For those who led a spiritual life, each moment brought some duty to be faithfully accomplished. Their whole attention was thus concentrated consecutively like a hand that marks the hours which, at each moment, traverses the space allotted to it. Their minds, incessantly animated by the impulsion of divine grace, turned imperceptibly to each new duty that presented itself by the permission of God at different hours of the day.[14]

Because in contemporary thought "duty" implies a burdensome responsibility, often unfairly imposed, placing de Caussade's use of the term within the context of divine love provides a necessary corrective. It also demonstrates the importance of the sacrament of the present moment as it pertains to servant spirituality. If, in the present moment, we perceive the suffering Christ in others, then our duty, arising from that perception, is an act of love, and that act of love is nothing less than authentic Christian service. Without the sacrament of the present moment, without recognizing Christ throughout our day, we pass right by Him. He goes unseen in our hearts, unnoticed in our ministry, and ultimately unappreciated in our lives. For those called to servant spirituality, sensitivity to the sacrament of the present moment is made possible through an ongoing encounter with the Servant Mysteries.

MEDITATIONS AND REFLECTIONS

As discussed earlier, this final section is designed to allow a deeper, more personal absorption of the material just covered. It consists of a set of two interrelated spiritual exercises whose sole purpose is to reengage the key themes in this chapter so as to internalize the truths they contain. This approach is based on the fundamental conviction that by prayerfully reflecting and meditating on these truths, God wants to speak to you in a way that will draw you into a deeper, more intimate communion with Christ the Servant. Each exercise should begin with at least a minute or two of relaxed silence, disposing your heart to the encounter. This should be followed by either a short extemporaneous prayer or, if you choose, the following:

> *Heavenly Father, I open my heart up to You so that, through the power of Your most Holy Spirit, I may encounter Your Son, Christ the Servant, in a deeply personal and transformative way. Forgive my sins and free me from the attachments of this world so that I am better attentive to Your presence and, in this attentiveness, hear what You want me to hear. Give me the grace to abandon myself to You in this moment for, in the depths of my soul, I want nothing more than You. Speak Lord, your servant listens. Mary, Mother of Christ the Servant, pray for me. Amen.*

KEY THEMES

The following represent some key themes found in this chapter. As you reflect on them, consider what Christ the Servant is revealing about Himself and, more importantly, what He's revealing about you. In this you're asking two distinct but related questions: Lord, what are you saying *in general* and, flowing from this, what are You saying specifically *to me*. Ponder how what is said may impact your relationship to Him, and how this may influence your relationship with others, particularly in the choices you make. Remember, as you meditate upon these things, to write down your thoughts in your journal or spiritual notebook. This may be a single word, a sentence, a paragraph, or even more. The purpose here is to capture the most important elements of your meditation, even if they are not whole or complete.

Recall that what is offered in these exercises is by way of a pious recommendation. You are free to fully engage or completely omit them as you see fit. Should you decide to move forward, you may take on one, some, or even all of the themes as the Spirit prompts you. This exercise and its effectiveness rely on grace and your openness to that grace. With all of this in mind, the key themes are as follows:

- The necessity of surrender
- Awareness of the ever-present God
- God as being itself
- Distinctions among public, private, and personal revelation
- The sacrament of the present moment
- Duty arising out of the present moment

REFLECTION QUESTIONS

Now that you have meditated upon these themes and captured what Christ the Servant may be saying to you, you can explore them further in the following six reflection questions. It's recommended that this be done in a separate sitting, giving you a chance to digest the fruit of your initial meditation. Should you choose to follow this recommendation, begin again with silence and prayer as described above. As with the key themes, write down your insights and thoughts in your journal or spiritual notebook.

- Identify two or three things you learned from this chapter that you didn't know before.

- Identify two or three key insights you gained through this chapter into your spiritual life, family, God, or the Church.
- Identify two or three ideas to apply your learning and insights from this chapter to your life as a Catholic.
- How might reading this chapter and reflecting on the key themes found within it deepen your *relationship to Christ the Servant*?
- How might reading this chapter and reflecting on the key themes found within it deepen your *identity in Christ the Servant*?
- How might reading this chapter and reflecting on the key themes found within it deepen your *mission with Christ the Servant*?

Chapter Four
The Servant Mysteries

These mysteries, truly Christ's own heart, define the deacon's ecclesial and spiritual life. Christ opens his heart to press its servant mysteries into the heart of the deacon, imbuing the man with a defining sacramental character.
Deacon James Keating, ***The Heart of the Diaconate: Communion with the Servant Mysteries of Christ***

As noted earlier, the Servant Mysteries are the revelation of Christ the Servant as made known in the Scriptures, Tradition, and, in particular, the sacrament of the present moment. They're everyday encounters found in prayer and ministry, in work and play, and indeed in all aspects of life, disclosing the true meaning of authentic Christian servanthood. These mysteries are most fully revealed in the passion, death, and resurrection of Jesus Christ. Far more than a specific kind of sacred knowledge, these mysteries offer insight into the person and mission of Jesus Christ, inviting those called to a servant spirituality into a more intimate communion with Him. In this respect, the Servant Mysteries are fundamentally relational. They enable us, as we draw closer to our Master, to grow in our vocation, bearing witness to Christ the Servant in concrete and tangible ways.

According to the *Basic Norms for the Formation of Permanent Deacons*, "The element which most characterises diaconal spirituality is the discovery of, and sharing in, the love of Christ the Servant, who came not to be served but to serve."[1] Given the intrinsic relationship between diaconal and servant spirituality, this is equally true of the laity. When actively engaged through divine abandonment, the Servant Mysteries are revealed in the sacrament of the present moment and, in these moments, Christ the Servant is encountered. As expressed beautifully by St. Thérèse of Lisieux, "Abandonment alone brings me / into your arms, O Jesus." These encounters, in turn, capacitate us to mystically identify with Him, to fall in love with Him, to be transformed by Him, and then, and only then, to serve Him. To better sensitize ourselves to these mysteries and the role they play in a servant spirituality, we will consider some of their key characteristics.

CHARACTERISTICS OF THE SERVANT MYSTERIES

As the Servant Mysteries become more and more a part of our interiority, the transformation that follows reveals that, while we became a servant of Christ at our Baptism, we are, in a certain sense, always becoming a servant. We are, as long as we actively and continually engage these mysteries, growing in our servanthood. This growth, in turn, sets up an abiding presence such that we become keenly aware of the needs around us and can better respond to them like the good and faithful servant we're called to be (Mt 25:21). For us to do so, we're called to model ourselves after the *Diakonos,* Jesus Christ. This requires an encounter with the Servant Mysteries. In what follows, we will consider seven characteristics of being a good servant as "points of departure" for ongoing reflection, meditation, and even contemplation. This is not meant to be an exhaustive list, nor are they given in any particular order. They simply highlight some of the more important aspects of Christ's servanthood.

Jesus Is the Model of a Good Servant: Jesus self-identifies as a servant among the people. "For who is greater: the one seated at table or the one who serves? Is it not the one seated at table? I am among you as the one who serves" (Lk 22:27). In his letter to the Romans, Saint Paul recognizes Jesus as deacon when he writes, "For I say that Christ became a minister [*diakonos*] of the circumcised to show God's truthfulness, to confirm the promises to the patriarchs" (Rom 15:8). Jesus fulfills His messianic mission through service, and that service finds its greatest expression in His passion, death, and resurrection. He reveals in His example that authentic servanthood is grounded, not so much in service to the people but, first and foremost, in service to the Father. It's only in this service to the Father that He serves the people: "I came down from heaven not to do my own will but the will of the one who sent me" (Jn 6:38). Servanthood, in this respect, is nothing less than an exercise of love — love of God and love of neighbor. It's both an expression and fulfillment of the Greatest Commandment (Mt 22:35–40; Mk 12:28–31; Lk 10:25–28; Jn 13:31–35).

Jesus' *Diakonia* **Is Rooted in Sacrificial Love:** The preeminent way in which Jesus acts as servant is by giving His life for the redemption of the world. "[T]he Son of Man did not come to be served but to serve and to give his life as a ransom for many" (Mt 20:28; cf. Mk 10:45; Jn 13:1–7). This service, expressed in unconditional self-giving, is revealed as a divine love outpoured. "No one has greater love than this, to lay down one's life for one's friends" (Jn 15:13). This divine love, expressed in human acts, motivates Jesus to His core. It inspires Him to abandon Himself to the Father by relinquishing His own will and adopting the will of the Father — even when this will entail great suffering: "Father, if you are willing, take this cup away from me; still, not my will but yours be done" (Lk 22:42). This act of love, an act by which all other loves are measured, demonstrates the sacrificial quality of Christ's love and, by extension, reveals the sacrificial quality of diaconal ministry.

Jesus' Love Sanctifies Believers: It's instructive to note that the English word *sacrifice* is made up of two Latin words: the verb *facere* which means "to make," and the noun *sanctus*, which means "holy." This means that to love sacrificially is to make holy not only the one being loved, but the one who loves; not only the one being served, but the one who serves. This is the transformative power of grace. In the biblical sense, holiness refers to a state of being set apart from sin and set apart for God. Sacrificial love consecrates those who actively participate in it. Understood this way, servant spirituality, when exercised sacrificially, has the potential to sanctify and in this respect contributes to the Mystery of Salvation.

Servanthood Requires a Willingness to Suffer for Others: I often joke with my students that one of my favorite theologians, Lou Costello (of Abbot and Costello fame), observed that marriage is a three-ring circus. First comes the engagement ring, then the wedding ring, then the suffering. Sadly, today's students haven't a clue of what is arguably one of the best comedy teams of all time. Still, imbued in much of their humor, indeed, in much of all humor, is truth expressed in an absurdity. In this case, the truth is that because marriage is rooted in love, it always entails sacrifice, and this sacrifice is often expressed in a kind of suffering. This is not only true of marital love but, to a greater or lesser degree, in all forms of love. If servant spirituality is a participation in the love of Christ the Servant, it will entail, as we've already seen, a degree of suffering. In this regard, the words of the Prophet Isaiah as applied to the Suffering Servant are of particular relevance:

> He was spurned and avoided by men, a man of suffering, knowing pain … and we held him in no esteem. Yet it was our pain that he bore, our sufferings he endured. We thought of him as stricken, struck down by God and afflicted, but he was pierced for our sins, crushed for our iniquity. He bore the punishment that makes us whole, by his wounds we were healed. (Isaiah 53:3–5)

For suffering to have a sacrificial value, it must be suffering for someone. It must be intentionally applied. The mere endurance of pain and heartache itself is not, in a strict sense, suffering. It's only when this pain, this heartache, is offered up *in union with the sufferings of Christ*, that it gains a redemptive value. It's Christ's suffering that makes our suffering salvific. Indeed, our suffering is but a vague reflection of, a pale imitation of, God's overwhelming suffering for us. When intentionally applied to Christ's redemptive suffering, our suffering becomes redemptive. It draws us closer to Him.

A Servant Is an Ambassador: We've already seen in the work of Collins that the deacon is a kind of emissary or ambassador. The same is true of the laity as they live out their baptismal promises, albeit in a different sense. They too are emissaries or ambassadors within the context of their particular vocation and state in life. Far from being menial, it's a position of great honor and dignity, deriving that honor from their relationship with the One who sends them. Because of that relationship, the emissary is entrusted with a critical mission. This mission requires him to go in the place of the One who sends him, with the authority of the One who sends him and, in conveying His message, convey His will. Of this Jesus says, "I came down from heaven not to do my own will but the will of the one who sent me" (Jn 6:38). Because He shares in the divine nature with the Father and the Spirit, He is both the One who sends and the One sent. By this fact, He is the *Diakonos*, communicating the will of the Father with an absolute degree of perfection. He is the Word-made-Flesh and, as such, the envoy *par excellence*, the perfect revelation of the One who sends Him. Because of this, He is the Emissary from which all emissaries derive their identity and mission.

One of the essential characteristics of being a good emissary is complete fidelity to the One who has sent him and to the mission with which he's been entrusted. He doesn't add to it or detract from it (Rv 22:18–19). Such fidelity requires, as a fundamental precondition, a kind of self-emptying or *kenosis* in which the envoy humbles himself, "becoming obedient to death, even death on a cross" (Phil 2:8). All ambassadors, upon receiving their respective missions, move from the one who sends them toward the ones to whom they are being sent. This initial movement, for Jesus, was accomplished through the Incarnation. This required a kind of self-emptying, such that He was to take on humanity fully, while at the same time remaining fully divine. In a similar, albeit human fashion, for ambassadors to remain faithful to the one who sends them, and to the mission with which they're tasked, they must empty themselves. This is only possible through a cultivation of the interior life. Here they come to know and love the One Who sends them through a form of divine abandonment. Abandonment to Christ, in the Servant Mysteries, constitutes a form of *kenosis*. By reflecting this love in carrying out their mission, envoys bring to life not only the message they bear, but the One who sends them as well. This is not possible without being faithful.

***Service Inspires Servanthood*:** Since Jesus' servanthood is the ultimate expression of divine love, and because love evokes, in the heart of the beloved, a reciprocal response, then Jesus' service inspires servanthood in those He serves. As we've already discussed, this love isn't some *thing*. It is some *One*; a gift of Himself, expressed in the offer of a shared life. The deep tenderness and profound compassion with which this gift is freely offered, and the unworthiness of the one to whom it's offered, wound the beloved to his core, moving him to say in the depths of his soul, "Lord, I am not worthy that you should come under my roof, but only say the word and my soul shall be healed" (cf. Mt. 8:8).

This gift, which comes as a result of a love freely offered and a love freely accepted, is not static, but possesses a dynamic quality. Jesus doesn't just give Himself on the cross for us, as though His passion remains merely an event fixed in time. True, it is historic in every respect, but at the very same time, its implications are timeless and eternal. Jesus' gift-of-self is expressed fully in the Paschal Mystery and resounds throughout history, resonating in the hearts of all who are willing to accept Him. This dynamic quality isn't limited to being trans-historic. It's also deeply personal. It's not a gift that is received once and then it's over; rather, it's continually received in the life of the believer. To use a common sentiment in an uncommon way, "Jesus is the Gift that keeps on giving." This gift, which is Love itself (1 Jn 4:8), in turn gives rise to a profound sense of gratitude; it moves the beloved to respond through his own gift-of-self, his own service, his own diaconate. What gives servant spirituality and the service that follows its unique quality is an *attitude of sacrificial gratitude*. This attitude finds its origins in the Last Supper, a supper which is inextricably linked to His service of redemption (Jn 13:1–35).

***Servanthood Restores the Proper Order*:** The *attitude of sacrificial gratitude* carries with it, as an essential component, the virtue of humility. The term *humility* is derived from the Latin word *humus* meaning "earth," and it indicates "the earth which is beneath us." This implies an interior disposition that is meek and servile.

In his classic work *The Twelve Degrees of Humility and of Pride*, St. Bernard of Clairvaux defines humility as "a virtue by which a man knowing himself as he truly is, abases himself." Similarly, St. Thomas Aquinas, in his *Summa contra Gentiles*, defines it as that which "consists in keeping oneself within one's own bounds, not reaching out to things above, but submitting to one's superior." In both cases, what is not implied is a kind of corruption or a loss of dignity. Such a negative connotation, often associated with various Protestant theologies, is completely inconsistent with Christ's service of redemption, which presupposes a humanity worth assuming and, more to the point, worth dying for.

Humility, applied here, means knowing our rightful place before God. This means that He's Creator, and we're created. He's Redeemer, and we're redeemed. He's Sanctifier, and we're sanctified. Likewise, with regard to servant spirituality, He's Servant, and we're servant. Knowing our rightful place within the divine order of things means we assume that place, and that place alone. This provides a necessary corrective to a corrupt form of service that seeks to oppress others by unduly subordinating them. Of this Jesus says:

> You know that the rulers of the Gentiles lord it over them, and the great ones make their authority over them felt. But it shall not be so among you. Rather, whoever wishes to be great among you shall be your servant; whoever wishes to be first among you shall be your slave. Just so, the Son of Man did not come to be served but to serve and to give his life as a ransom for many. (Matthew 20:25–28)

The above characteristics represent a sampling of sorts designed to familiarize the reader with what makes the Servant Mysteries what they are. While not complete, they do reveal that the Servant Mysteries point to and make present the Servant Mystery, Jesus Christ. He's the *Typos*, the Exemplar, the Pattern upon which the Servant Mysteries find their meaning and purpose. Indeed, when we, through servant spirituality, configure ourselves to the Servant Mysteries, we at the very same time conform ourselves to the Servant Mystery, Christ Jesus. In doing so, we too, in a derivative way, become servant mysteries in our own lives, revealing the love of God and extending the gift of salvation.

A BEAUTY THAT WOUNDS

> *It will happen that while the soul is inflamed with the Love of God, it will feel that a seraph is assailing it by means of an arrow or dart which is all afire with love. And the seraph pierces and in an instant cauterizes [burns] this soul, which, like a red-hot coal, or better a flame, is already enkindled. The soul is converted into an immense fire of Love.*
> **St. John of the Cross on the Transverberation of St. Teresa of Ávila's Heart**

In his book *The Heart of the Diaconate*, Deacon James Keating speaks of the Servant Mysteries as Christ's own heart "pressed" into the heart of the deacon at ordination.[2] This "impression" is nothing less than an intense encounter that forever changes him. In what at first seems rather strange language, Keating describes ordination as a kind of deep wounding. In this wounding — which speaks to an intimate encounter — the deacon's heart is lacerated by Christ's own beauty and the beauty of His mission.

This intimacy is lovingly expressed by St. John of the Cross, who writes, "For when this flame of divine life wounds the soul with the gentle languishing for the life of God, it wounds it with so much endearing tenderness, and softens it so that it melts away in love."[3] This way of speaking only makes sense when ordination, and indeed the whole of the diaconate, is understood within the context of a deep intimate communion with Christ the Servant.

While the laity do not share in this same kind of wounding arising from ordination, they nonetheless are wounded in Baptism and Confirmation. Because there is only one Christ, the one Christ who wounds during ordination to the diaconate also wounds during Baptism and Confirmation, albeit in a lay sense. This means that the laity are, through a kind of wounding proper to their specific vocation, configured to Christ who is a servant. They do not receive the same sanctifying grace that a deacon does by virtue of his ordination to bear witness to Christ the Servant in a preeminent way. However, they do receive grace to serve, though in a more general sense, thereby extending the witness of Christ the Servant in their lives and the lives of those they touch. This means that one of the definitive qualities of a servant spirituality is to purify and, as we shall see, keep open these wounds, sustaining the initial encounter and, with it, the grace to serve others.

To better appreciate this notion of woundedness, it would be helpful to use the analogy of marriage. In marriage, a husband, deeply in love with his wife, is wounded by her inner beauty. He sees in her something so precious that he's driven to his knees, injured, so to speak, by her profound loveliness. Popular romantic terms such as longing, pining, and yearning all bespeak the kind of suffering that comes from a woundedness inflicted by her beauty. A similar illustration occurs on Saint Valentine's Day with a heart pierced by an arrow. Here, it's important to recognize that this kind of beauty isn't mere physical allure, but something much deeper. It concerns the attractiveness of her entire being, such that her being makes up what is missing in him. She fulfills an emptiness, and her presence brings a kind of consolation and satisfaction. Consequently, what is desired isn't something about her, some desirable trait, but simply her. The perception of this inner beauty enables him to glimpse, ever-so-slightly, what God sees in her, and that inner sight far exceeds any physical quality, no matter how sensually attractive that quality may be. This is why, as his wife grows older, she becomes even more beautiful to him, despite the effects of age. Reflecting on this kind of beauty and the woundedness it brings, Cardinal Joseph Ratzinger (now Pope Emeritus Benedict XVI) wrote:

> For Plato, beauty in fact is a cause of suffering. The encounter with it comes as a shock which takes the individual out of his everyday existence and nurtures in him a longing for the original perfection that was conceived for him and which he has since lost. The shock of the encounter with beauty is like an arrow that pierces man, wounds him and in this way gives him wings, lifts him upwards toward the transcendent. ... The longing elicited by beauty finds its healing, through the revelation of the New Testament, in the Truth which redeems. ... When men have a longing so great that it passes human nature ... it's the Bridegroom himself who has wounded them. Into their eyes he himself has sent a ray of beauty.[4]

Like the diaconate, albeit in a lay sense, the laity are wounded by Christ's inner beauty, particularly as that beauty is revealed in the Servant Mysteries through the sacrament of the present moment. They see in these mysteries a Servant so precious that they're driven to their knees, injured, so to speak, by the outpouring of this Servant's love for humanity and for them. This is precisely what Saint Augustine meant when he observed, "In my deepest wound I saw your glory and it dazzled me."[5] As the laity allow Christ to draw close, particularly through the Servant Mysteries, His Divine Presence reveals an emptiness within them, a place that Christ the Servant, and only Christ the Servant, can fill. So, prior to this encounter in Baptism and Confirmation, and even after, they long, pine, and yearn for this fulfillment — and this bespeaks the kind of suffering that comes from a woundedness inflicted by Christ's beauty. Because this fulfillment won't reach its perfection until they stand before the throne of God and are judged worthy, this woundedness, and the suffering that accompanies it, will last throughout their lives, bringing with it a fulfillment that's never quite fulfilled, a satisfaction that's never quite satisfied.

Here, what attracts isn't something about Christ — it's not simply some aspect of His life, passion, death, and resurrection — but instead something much deeper. It concerns the attractiveness of His entire being, such that His being makes up what is missing in the person. Christ the Servant fulfills an emptiness, and His Divine Presence brings a kind of consolation that overcomes any desolation. Consequently, what is desired isn't something about Christ, some desirable trait, some aspect of His ministry, but simply Him. The perception of this inner beauty enables the laity to glimpse, ever-so-slightly, God, and that inner sight far exceeds any aspect of Christ's life, no matter how profound that aspect may be. This is why, as a lay person progresses in the interior life over the years, Christ the Servant becomes even more beautiful to him or her, despite the trials and hardships often associated with the Christian life.

Ordinarily, we think of wounding as something negative, and in many respects it certainly can be. This negative kind of wounding is characterized by a malicious intent, often accompanied by physical or emotional violence. In situations like this, the one being wounded is treated as some kind of object to be used, possessed, and discarded at the end of the day. This negative wounding is antithetical to the kind of positive wounding found in such relationships as marriage. Positive wounding, on the other hand, is characterized by a beneficial intent accompanied by a deep consideration for the other. Here, the one being wounded, in this case the husband, isn't treated by the one wounding, his wife, as an object to be used, but rather as a person to be loved, respected, and valued. In this case, the husband, so moved by the beauty of the wife, doesn't desire to possess her as in negative wounding, but instead, to be possessed by her. In this dynamic, love moves between the husband and wife in a mutual way, such that both allow themselves to be wounded by the other.

Likewise, the wounding received in Baptism and Confirmation, and lived throughout the Christian life, is characterized by a beneficial intent accompanied by a deep consideration for the other. Here the one wounded isn't treated by the One wounding as an object to be used, but rather as a person to be respected and valued. This person, so moved by the beauty of Christ the Servant, doesn't desire to possess Him, but instead, to be possessed by Him. In this dynamic, love moves between the person and Christ in a mutual way, such that both allow themselves to be wounded by the other.

For wounding to take place on the level of marriage, the beauty that attracts must be *unique and proper to the couple*. This happens when both recognize a calling, a vocation, to marry each other. The world is chock full of people who possess inner beauty, and while all of them are attractive in some way, only one can be chosen to share in the mutual woundedness that is marriage. In this case, woundedness is exclusive to one. Only one can be permitted to wound me, and certitude that this is the one comes when she desires to be wounded *by me*. In this respect, there's always a double wounding.

What gives the suffering associated with being wounded its nobility isn't the pain and hardship it brings but, as with Christ, the application of this pain and heartache to the salvation it offers. This is the only suitable response to the woundedness experienced because it's the only response capable of expressing the love felt. Beauty, woundedness, and suffering — as these relate to the laity and their vocation — draw them, and those they serve, into deep, intimate communion with Christ. They participate, each in their own way, in Christ's salvific mission; through this He extends His hands into the world through their lives of faith. Because they share in a unique way in Christ's own servanthood, they, wounded by Christ, now share in His suffering. They become, like their Master, a suffering servant.

The quality of suffering as it relates to Christian service, revealed by Christ, and witnessed by the diaconate, was foreshadowed by the Prophet Isaiah. In four distinct but related songs we learn that God will choose a servant to bring justice to the world, not by political or military action, but by working quietly and confidently to establish right religion. He will restore Israel, but not without cost and not without being wounded:

> He was spurned and avoided by men,
> > a man of suffering, knowing pain,
> Like one from whom you turn your face,
> > spurned, and we held him in no esteem.
> Yet it was our pain that he bore,
> > our sufferings he endured.
> We thought of him as stricken,
> > struck down by God and afflicted,
> but he was pierced for our sins,
> > crushed for our iniquity.
> He bore the punishment that makes us whole,

> by his wounds we were healed.
> My servant, the just one, shall justify the many. (Isaiah 53:3–5, 11)

The Scriptures directly identify Isaiah's Suffering Servant as Jesus. In the Acts of the Apostles, Saint Luke describes a meeting between the deacon Philip and an Ethiopian eunuch on the road from Jerusalem to Gaza. Philip asks, "Do you understand what you are reading?" to which the Ethiopian responds, "How can I, unless someone instructs me?" At this point, "Philip opened his mouth and, beginning with this Scripture passage, he proclaimed Jesus to him" (Acts 8:26–35). The Church has long seen Jesus as the Suffering Servant, so much so that the early Church Fathers dubbed the Suffering Servant Songs the "Fifth Gospel."

It's fascinating to observe that the first one to recognize and apply Isaiah's Suffering Servant to Christ is a deacon. One could speculate that, insofar as Philip was called to live out the Servant Mysteries, he recognized, in the experience of Christ's own suffering, a quality of service, an expression of divine love. Perhaps this quality resonated so profoundly within Philip's heart, having been wounded by Christ the Servant in his own call to *diakonia*, that he could reach no other conclusion when the Ethiopian eunuch asked, "I beg you, about whom is the prophet saying this?" (Acts 8:34). To this, "Philip opened his mouth and, beginning with this Scripture passage, he proclaimed Jesus to him" (Acts 8:35).

KEEPING THE WOUNDS OPEN

> *I do not desire to die soon, because in Heaven there is no suffering. I desire to live a long time because I yearn to suffer much for the love of my Spouse.*
> **St. Mary Magdalene de Pazzi, Letters**

Just as Christ's wounds remain open so that, beyond His own time, future generations may experience the saving effect of that woundedness, so too the deacon must, as Deacon Keating often points out, keep his wounds fresh so that he can effectively fulfill his mission.[6] In a similar way the laity, too, following the example of the diaconate, must keep their wounds open. In both cases, these wounds represent a kind of internal stigmata. As the stigmata is an outward sign of a participation in Christ's own woundedness and a sharing of His salvific mission, so too this wounding finds its source and strength in Christ the Servant.

St. Francis of Assisi, a deacon himself, bore the stigmata and, in doing so, manifested in his body what he was already suffering in his soul. Two years prior to his death, while in deep prayer on a remote mountaintop in La Verna, Italy, an angel representing Christ appeared to him mounted on a cross. At the request of Pope Gregory IX, Thomas of Celano later wrote an account of this event based on the testimony of the two friars that accompanied Francis. In it, he conveys:

> The marks of nails began to appear in his hands and feet, just as he had seen them slightly earlier in the crucified man above him. His wrists and feet seemed to be pierced by nails, with the heads of the nails appearing on his wrists and on the upper sides of his feet, the points appearing on the other side. ... In the same way the marks of nails were impressed on his feet and pro-

jected beyond the rest of the flesh. Moreover, his right side had a large wound as if it had been pierced with a spear.[7]

Once received, these wounds remained open for the rest of Francis's life. They reflected a life lived in intense communion with Christ the Servant, such that Jesus' sufferings became Francis's sufferings. Although few are called to experience this kind of heroic virtue on the outside, all Christians are called and graced to live it heroically on the inside. The extent to which the laity are open to acknowledging the interior stigmata received at Baptism and Confirmation, and the extent to which they seek to live this out in the sacrament of the present moment, is the extent to which Christ the Servant is revealed in their lives. While such a call carries with it all of the sufferings associated with the wounds, it's not without its consolations. Of Francis's wounds Saint Bonaventure later wrote, "The sight of it amazed Francis and his soul experienced joy mingled with pain. He was delighted with the sight of Christ appearing to him so graciously and intimately and ... [it] aroused in his soul a joy of compassionate love."[8]

Following the example of Saint Francis and embracing a servant spirituality, the primary way the laity keep open the wound is through a participation in the Servant Mysteries as they're revealed, first and foremost, in the interior life. Here, through deep prayer, meditation, and even contemplation, they encounter Christ the Servant whose beauty surpasses all others. When this encounter is genuinely sought in a state of grace, Jesus reaches out and touches them, and they, so moved by His beauty, are wounded. This woundedness arises out of an experience of being loved well beyond what they believe their worth to be, to be sent on a mission that far exceeds their natural capacities. Echoing the words of King David before God, they say "Who am I, Lord God, and what is my house, that you should have brought me so far?" (2 Sm 7:18).

This outpouring of divine love, through multiple encounters with Christ the Servant in the Servant Mysteries, keeps open the wounds. This woundedness then bleeds over into their life and ministry, bringing with it a humility proper to being a good and faithful servant. Returning again and again to the Servant Mysteries, they keep fresh this precious wound that enables them to suffer for Christ and, perhaps more to the point, to suffer well. Because the Servant Mysteries represent their ongoing encounters with Christ the Servant, they represent the very soul of Christian service. Just as our soul infuses the body, giving it life, so too the Servant Mysteries infuse the laity's vocation with new life. When they are faithful to these mysteries, they become the living embodiment of them, rendering them radically capable of bearing witness to Christ the Servant.

As noted earlier, the Servant Mysteries are the revelation of Christ the Servant as made known in the sacrament of the present moment. As such, they play a critical role in servant spirituality because they allow the laity to encounter, in a constant and ongoing way, Christ the Servant, thereby keeping open the wounds received at Baptism and Confirmation. By meditating on these mysteries, particularly in their prayer and life, the laity come to realize a profound truth: that the Servant Mysteries don't simply mediate authentic servanthood but, as we've already observed, mediate Someone. Jesus Christ, the Son of the Living God, is the primordial Servant Mystery. Reflecting on these mysteries makes Him present in a profound way in the life of the deacon and, through his witness, in the life of the laity. Here, Christ the Servant becomes more real, His Presence more intense, His grace more palpable. These encounters transform the laity from the inside out such that they now become the living embodiment of the Servant Mysteries. This renders them radically capable of incarnating Christ the Servant, not just in the exercise of their vocation, but in every aspect of their lives. In this respect, the laity themselves become a servant mystery to others, and even to themselves.

APPLYING THE SACRAMENT OF THE PRESENT MOMENT

> *To be satisfied with the present moment is to delight in it, and to adore the divine will in all that has to be done or suffered in all that succession of events that fill, as they pass, each present moment.*
> **Jean-Pierre de Caussade,** *Abandonment to Divine Providence*

The Servant Mysteries, whose characteristics we explored earlier, are an essential component in a servant spirituality. They enable the faithful to grow in their vocation by bearing witness to Christ the Servant in their lives and vocations. With this in mind, we now turn to examine how the Servant Mysteries are to permeate and penetrate the entire life of the laity. We will do this by once again applying de Caussade's sacrament of the present moment. Recall that the sacrament of the present moment is the realization that the ever-present God makes Himself known to us through everyday events such as the people we meet, the places we go, and even in our struggles. It represents, as we've seen, a kind of personal revelation that is constant and ongoing. Unlike other kinds of personal revelation, it doesn't concern itself with some specific thing such as a vocation, job, or house, but instead focuses on an ongoing awareness of God's presence in the here and now.

Because they were configured to Christ the Servant at Baptism and Confirmation, it's Christ that calls the laity to Himself in and through the Servant Mysteries. In this respect, the Servant Mysteries don't simply reveal Christ the Servant; they make Him sacramentally present and, through Him, provide access to the inner life of the Trinity. Abandonment to divine providence, as applied to servant spirituality, means abandonment to Christ the Servant — which indicates a life that doesn't merely pray or meditate on the Servant Mysteries, but lives them out. In this, the faithful become, through a participation in the sanctifying grace proper to their state in life, a servant mystery themselves, revealing in their words and actions the Servant Mystery that is Christ Jesus.

By cultivating an interior life grounded in the Servant Mysteries, the faithful are drawn into a deep, interpersonal communion with Christ the Servant. Here, they're filled with a love that's not their own, given a vision that's not their own, and provided a strength that's not their own. Yet at the same time, that love, that vision, and that strength so imbue their lives, so wound them to their core, that these mysteries become their own, in a certain sense. This means that the Servant Mysteries are realized in the sacrament of the present moment regardless of where that moment takes place, whether it's the interior or exterior life, whether it's at prayer or in ministry, whether it's with their spouse or children.

This approach means not only bringing Christ the Servant to those we meet, but seeing Christ the Servant in those very same people. It might be asked, "How can this be? How do we at once be Him and, at the same time, see Him?" While it's certainly true that Christ isn't present to us as He was when He walked the earth some two thousand years ago, He is, nonetheless, sacramentally present in at least three ways. First, insofar as we are all created in the image of God and, insofar as Jesus is God, the image of Christ is present in everyone. Indeed, because the faithful, by virtue of their calling, are attuned to the Servant Mysteries, they see by default Christ the Servant. In Saint Matthew's "Judgment of the

Nations," Jesus speaks directly of this with respect to service:

> Then the king will say to those on his right, "Come, you who are blessed by my Father. Inherit the kingdom prepared for you from the foundation of the world. For I was hungry and you gave me food, I was thirsty and you gave me drink, a stranger and you welcomed me, naked and you clothed me, ill and you cared for me, in prison and you visited me." Then the righteous will answer him and say, "Lord, when did we see you hungry and feed you, or thirsty and give you drink? When did we see you a stranger and welcome you, or naked and clothe you? When did we see you ill or in prison, and visit you?" And the king will say to them in reply, "Amen, I say to you, whatever you did for one of these least brothers of mine, you did for me." (Matthew 25:34–40)

Second, we often see things in their absence, juxtaposing that which is there with that which is lacking. In those we serve, our sensitivity to Christ the Servant helps us move beyond the superficial to a deeper reality. We know, because of the intimacy we share with Christ the Servant, that suffering doesn't indicate the absence of God, but instead His presence. In this paradox, we encounter the love of God precisely in and through His suffering, such that suffering reveals Him and His great love for us in a way nothing else does. He is the Suffering Servant, present in those who suffer.

This paradox is poignantly illustrated by the Romanian-born American writer Elie Wiesel in his moving book *Night*. At the height of the Holocaust, a young Elie and his father were imprisoned in a Nazi concentration camp. He recalled, at one point, being forced to watch the hanging of a boy. The boy weighed so little that the noose failed to break his neck, agonizingly prolonging his death. Others were then forced to weigh him down by hanging on his feet. In the midst of this, Elie heard someone ask: "For God's sake, where is God?" Within him, he heard a voice respond saying, "Where is He? This is where — hanging here from this gallows."[9]

Finally, we see Christ the Servant reflected in the eyes of those we serve. Just as it's impossible to touch without simultaneously being touched, so too it's impossible to bring Christ the Servant without seeing a reflection of ourselves acting in the person of that same Christ. Of course, both cases require a modicum of interior attentiveness. This realization is particularly obvious when, after the completion of an aspect of our lives in which we have satisfied some need, we experience an internal satisfaction. This satisfaction arises because we have fulfilled the will of the One who sent us, completing our mission as emissaries. Figuratively speaking, in the reflection of the eyes of those we serve, we see the love of a good and faithful servant: We see ourselves acting as Christ the Servant. This reflection reveals not only what we are — servants — but more importantly, it affirms and strengthens our identity. It helps us to know we are doing the will of the One who sent us and, in a certain sense, incarnating Him by extending His hands from heaven to earth. In this respect, the faithful fulfill their role in the Mystery of Salvation. They become more fully what they are.

PRAYER OF ABANDONMENT AND LITTLE EXAMEN

> *If we neglect prayer and if the branch is not connected with the vine, it will die. That connecting of the branch to the vine is prayer. If that connection is there then love is there, then joy is there, and we will be the sunshine of God's love, the hope of eternal happiness, the flame of burning love. Why? Because we are one with Jesus.*
> **St. Teresa of Calcutta**

The rich spiritual and mystical tradition of the Church offers a treasure trove of devout practices, and divine abandonment represents only one of these. All require a certain level of discernment before they are undertaken. All involve considerable effort to maintain. All have similar pitfalls with regard to our steadfastness. No matter what we choose, it's really God who chooses us. Thus, the grace necessary to persevere will be given, guaranteed (2 Cor 12:9)! That said, no spiritual practice is perfect this side of heaven. God doesn't call the perfect, only those willing to be perfected.

If, in prayer, we sense God may be calling us to divine abandonment as described in this book, and if, in conversation with our spiritual director, confessor, or trusted companion in the Faith, this is confirmed, then we ought to begin a discernment process. There's no better way to discern a spiritual practice then by actually taking it up on a temporary basis. Whether you decide to move forward with divine abandonment on a temporary or continual basis, the spiritual exercises as recommended here are hardly burdensome. They already presume, because you picked up this book, that you're currently praying on a regular basis and perhaps even have other long-held devotions such as adoration, *lectio divina*, or the Rosary. In this respect, they're meant to augment your prayers with a specialized prayer of abandonment and a little examen respectively. These prayers are meant to catalyze our lives with a greater sensitivity to the Servant Mysteries as they are revealed in the sacrament of the present moment, be it in the interior or exterior dimensions of our lives. If we are to live out the Servant Mysteries and become Christ the Servant to others, it will be necessary, as St. John Vianney points out, to stretch ourselves:

> My little children, your hearts are small, but prayer stretches them and makes them capable of loving God. Through prayer we receive a foretaste of heaven and something of paradise comes down upon us. Prayer never leaves us without sweetness. It is honey that flows into the soul and makes all things sweet. When we pray properly, sorrows disappear like snow before the sun.[10]

The Morning Prayer of Abandonment is drawn from the diaconal prayer of ordination and has been modified for use by the laity. It may be said at the beginning of each day along with the prayers you already pray. Just as Jesus is the Primordial Servant Mystery and was manifested at our Baptism and Confirmation where He configured us to Himself, the Prayer of Abandonment harkens back to those moments, making them sacramentally present at the start of our day. It draws upon the supernatural abundant storehouse of grace given to us when we received the gift of Christ the Servant.

MORNING PRAYER OF ABANDONMENT

> *Almighty God, be present with me by Your power. You are the source of all my honor, You assign me my place, You give me my vocation.*

So that I may grow in greater intimacy with You, and serve you in love and fidelity, I abandon my day, my hour, and indeed every moment of my life to You, Father, Son and Holy Spirit.

Free me from the snares of the Evil One and the attachments of this world, that I may always be what You want me to be, go where You want me to go, and do what You want me to do.

Help me to see You in the needs of those who suffer and to reach beyond my own limitations, making You present in the exercise of the gift of my faith. Make me ever conscious of the Servant Mysteries in the sacrament of the present moment so that I may excel in every virtue: in love that is sincere, in concern for the sick and the poor, in unassuming authority, in self-discipline, and in holiness in life.

May I remain strong and steadfast in Christ, giving to the world the witness of a pure conscience. May I in this life imitate Your Son, who came not to be served but to serve, and one day reign with Him in heaven. I ask this through Christ our Lord. Amen.

Mary, Mother of God, exemplar of Christian service, pray for me that I may serve Your Son by serving others. (Say three times.)

Whereas the Prayer of Abandonment starts our day, the Little Examen ends it. They are designed to work together, fixing our gaze firmly on Christ the Servant. The Little Examen isn't meant to replace a formal examination of conscience. If it's your practice to do a daily examination, I suggest you don't relinquish it, but instead incorporate the Little Examen into it. I call this the Little Examen as, like the Prayer of Abandonment, it's not meant to supplant our current prayer routine but supplement it. It's short and sweet, but in its brevity and simplicity it enables us to reflect back upon our day, acknowledging our successes and failures as they pertain to our abandonment. For the successes, for the times we became aware of the Servant Mysteries in the sacrament of the present moment, we give God thanks and praise, for its only by responding to His grace that such an awareness is possible. Likewise, for the times when we've missed Him or even sought to avoid Him, we ask for His pardon and peace. The Prayer of Abandonment and the Little Examen work in conjunction with one another to help better cultivate the interior life as servants of the Lord.

LITTLE EXAMEN

Almighty God, at the close of this day I turn to You in complete abandonment. I beg You, send Your Holy Spirit upon me that I may now enter Your peace, calling to mind my sins and shortcomings.

Brief period of silence
- Have I made a conscious effort today to perceive You in the sacrament of the present moment?
- Where have I seen You, and how did I respond to Your presence?
- Where have I missed You?
- Where have I deliberately ignored You?
- For the times I was aware of Your presence in the lives of those I encountered, I give You thanks and praise. For the times I failed to see You, and for the times I failed to respond to Your needs, I am truly sorry.
- So that I may grow in greater intimacy with You and

better bear witness to the world through the gift of my vocation, I ask Your pardon and peace.

Pray an Act of Contrition.

O my God, I am heartily sorry for having offended Thee, and I detest all my sins because of Thy just punishments, but most of all because they offend Thee, my God, who art all good and deserving of all my love. I firmly resolve with the help of Thy grace to sin no more and to avoid the near occasion of sin. Amen.

Mary, Mother of God, exemplar of Christian service, pray for me that I may serve your Son by serving others. (Say three times.)

MEDITATIONS AND REFLECTIONS

As observed earlier, this final section is designed to allow a deeper, more personal absorption of the material just covered. It consists of a set of two interrelated spiritual exercises whose sole purpose is to reengage the key themes in this chapter so as to internalize the truths they contain. This approach is based on the fundamental conviction that by prayerfully reflecting and meditating on these truths, God wants to speak to you in a way that will draw you into a deeper, more intimate communion with Christ the Servant. Each exercise should begin with at least a minute or two of relaxed silence, disposing your heart to the encounter. This should be followed by either a short extemporaneous prayer or, if you choose, the following:

Heavenly Father, I open my heart up to You so that, through the power of Your most Holy Spirit, I may encounter Your Son, Christ the Servant, in a deeply personal and transformative way. Forgive my sins and free me from the attachments of this world so that I am better attentive to Your presence and, in this attentiveness, hear what You want me to hear. Give me the grace to abandon myself to You in this moment for, in the depths of my soul, I want nothing more than You. Speak, Lord, Your servant listens. Mary, Mother of Christ the Servant, pray for me. Amen.

KEY THEMES

The following represent some key themes found in this chapter. As you reflect on them, consider what Christ the Servant is revealing about Himself and, more importantly, what He's revealing about you. In this you're asking two distinct but related questions: Lord, what are You saying *in general* and, flowing from this, what are You saying specifically *to me*. Ponder how what is said may impact your relationship to Him, and how this may influence your relationship with others, particularly in the choices you make. Remember, as you meditate upon these things, to write down your thoughts in your journal or spiritual notebook. This may be a single word, a sentence, a paragraph, or even more. The purpose here is to capture the most important elements of your meditation, even if they are not whole or complete.

Recall that what is offered in these exercises is by way of a pious recommendation. You are free to fully engage or completely omit them as you see fit. Should you decide to move forward, you may take on one, some, or even all of the themes as the Spirit prompts you. This exercise and its effectiveness rely on grace and your openness to that grace. With all of this in mind, the key themes are as follows:

- Characteristics of the Servant Mysteries
- The beauty that wounds
- The difference between positive and negative

wounding
- Keeping the wounds open
- Applying the Servant Mysteries to the sacrament of the present moment
- Integrating the Prayer of Abandonment and Little Examen into my daily prayer routine

REFLECTION QUESTIONS

Now that you have meditated upon these themes and captured what Christ the Servant may be saying to you, you can explore them further in the following six reflection questions. It's recommended that this be done in a separate sitting, giving you a chance to digest the fruit of your initial meditation. Should you choose to follow this recommendation, begin again with silence and prayer as described above. As with the key themes, write down your insights and thoughts in your journal or spiritual notebook.

- Identify two or three things you learned from this chapter that you didn't know before.
- Identify two or three key insights you gained through this chapter into your spiritual life, family, God, or the Church.
- Identify two or three ideas to apply your learning and insights from this chapter to your life as a Catholic.
- How might reading this chapter and reflecting on the key themes found within it deepen your *relationship to Christ the Servant*?
- How might reading this chapter and reflecting on the key themes found within it deepen your *identity in Christ the Servant*?
- How might reading this chapter and reflecting on the key themes found within it deepen your *mission with Christ the Servant*?

Final Thoughts

Spread love everywhere you go: first of all in your own house. Give love to your children, to your wife or husband, to a next door neighbor. ... Let no one ever come to you without leaving better and happier. Be the living expression of God's kindness; kindness in your face, kindness in your eyes, kindness in your smile, kindness in your warm greeting.

St. Teresa of Calcutta

By responding to a divine call, the faithful enter into a new and more intimate relationship with Christ the Servant. In this relationship, we find not only our identity but our mission as well. Inspired and informed by Christ's gift-of-self received at Baptism and strengthened in Confirmation, God empowers us to live out our vocations in a way that actualizes our identity through sacred service, the definitive characteristic of which is a gift-of-self that wills the good of the other for the sake of the other. Thus, each of us finds within us a summons that we cannot ignore, one that specifies our relationship to, our identity in, and our mission with Christ the Servant. It's a summons that can be expressed and realized in the phrase, "Servants of Christ, become what you are."

If authentic renewal of the faithful is to take place — if we are to become more fully what we are — it must begin with a rediscovery of the interior life, rooted in a more complete theology of service and realized in a corresponding spirituality. Indeed, insofar as theology is in service to the spiritual life, this theology, when personally appropriated, can only serve to deepen our interior communion with Christ the Servant, further refining our identity and, in the process, rendering our lives more meaningful. Together, the Establishment Hypothesis, along with RIM, provide the theological basis and the spiritual structure to better integrate our interior and exterior lives. It enables us, in the very living out of our vocations, to experience Christ the Servant and, in Him, a little heaven on earth. This is, in the end, what a lay spirituality of service is all about.

Finally, this work would not be complete without commending it to the intercession of the Blessed Virgin Mary. Her example of humble service bore Christ the Servant, giving us its perfect model. Beyond that, insofar as she is the mother of Christ the Servant, and insofar as we are configured to that same Christ, she isn't only His mother in the order of sacred service, but ours as well. With this in mind, to her many titles two more can be added: *Mary, Mother of the Diaconate* and *Mary, Mother of Christ the Servant.* This is a title not only proper to deacons, but to all of the faithful called to follow the example of Christ the servant. As St. Maximilian Kolbe reminds us, "Never be afraid of loving the Blessed Virgin too much. You can never love her more than Jesus did." Joining our voice to hers, let us always respond to the call of the Holy Spirit by saying, "We are the servants of the Lord, let it be done to us according to His word."

Sancta Maria, Mater Diaconati, ora pro nobis.

Notes

INTRODUCTION: THE SEARCH FOR INTIMACY

1. Francis Thompson, "The Hound of Heaven," in *The Hound of Heaven: A Modern Adaptation,* ed. Greg Bandy (California: Emblem Media, 2014), Kindle location 146.

2. Dominic Cerrato, "The Indispensability of the Diaconate: Toward a More Integrated Understanding of the Origins of Holy Orders and God's Plan of Salvation," *Josephinum Diaconal Review* (Spring 2017), 36.

3. Though the primary responsibility of this falls to the local bishop, it is naturally delegated to the diaconate. Congregation for Catholic Education, *Basic Norms for the Formation of Permanent Deacons,* 16.

4. John Paul II, *Familiaris consortio,* par. 11.

5. OSV has many excellent books that cover foundational topics of the Catholic Faith. Among them are *Believe Celebrate Live Pray: A Weekly Walk with the Catechism* by Jem Sullivan; *How to Pray: A Practical Guide to the Spiritual Life* by David Torkington; *The Handy Little Guide to Confession* by Michelle Jones Schroeder; and *A Pocket Guide to the Mass* by Michael Dubruiel.

6. *Catechism of the Catholic Church,* par. 2705.

7. Ignatius of Loyola, in *The Quotable Saint,* ed. Rosemary Ellen Guiley (New York: Facts On File, Inc., 2002), 173.

8. Fulton J. Sheen, *Life of Christ* (New York: Image Books, 1977), 213.

9. Francis Xavier, *The Life and Letters of Saint Francis Xavier,* vol. 2, ed. Henry James Coleridge (London: Burns & Oates, 1872), 433.

CHAPTER ONE: A SPIRITUALITY ROOTED IN THE DIACONATE

1. Dominic Cerrato, James Keating, et. al., "Diaconal Formation within Priestly Formation," *Josephinum Diaconal Review* (Fall 2019): 4–14.

2. John N. Collins, *Diakonia: Re-Interpreting Ancient Sources* (New York: Oxford University Press, 1990).

3. Ibid., 195–215.

4. "Similarly, deacons must be dignified, not deceitful, not addicted to drink, not greedy for sordid gain, holding fast to the mystery of the faith with a clear conscience. Moreover, they should be tested first; then, if there is nothing against them, let them serve as deacons. Women, similarly, should be dignified, not slanderers, but temperate and faithful in everything. Deacons may be married only once and must manage their children and their households well. Thus those who serve well as deacons gain good standing and much confidence in their faith in Christ Jesus" (1 Tm 3:8–13).

5. It's not at all necessary for the lay reader to read the two prior books to fully appreciate servant spirituality. Much of what is found in those books has been incorporated, albeit in an abridged way, into this book.

6. John F. Crosby, *The Personalism of John Paul II* (Steubenville, OH: Hildebrand Press, 2019), 1–8.

7. Dominic Cerrato, *In the Person of Christ the Servant: A Theology of the Diaconate Based on the Personalist Thought of Pope John Paul II* (Bloomingdale, OH: St. Ephraem Press, 2014), 190–207.

8. *Compendium of the Catechism of the Catholic Church* (Washington, D.C.: United States Conference of Catholic Bishops, 2006), 34.

9. Thomas Aquinas, *Summa Theologica*, II-II, q.26, a.6.

10. *Gaudium et spes*, par. 24.

11. *Lumen Gentium*, par. 21b.

12. The stole is the vestment used to designate a man who has received Holy Orders. It's a long strip of material about four inches wide, and the manner in which it is worn signifies his rank. The stole is worn over the white undergarment (alb) and under the outer garment (chasuble for a priest and dalmatic for a deacon). It's only seen when the outer garments are not worn.

13. James Keating, *The Heart of the Diaconate: Communion with the Servant Mysteries of Christ* (Mahwah, NJ: Paulist Press, 2015), 64.

14. Cardinal Walter Kasper, "The Deacon Offers an Ecclesiological View of the Present-Day Challenges in the Church and Society" (lecture, IDC Study Conference, Brixen, Italy, October 1997).

15. Richard Gabuzda, "Relationship, Identity, Mission: A Proposal for Spiritual Formation," in *2005 Symposium, Interiority for Mission: Spiritual Formation for Priests of*

the New Evangelization, ed. Edward Mathews (Omaha: IPF Publications, 2005), 39–51.

16. Thomas Aquinas, *Boethius de trinitate*, 6,4, and 5, cited in Brian Mullady, *Man's Desire for God* (Bloomington: 1st Books, 2003), 19.

17. John Paul II, *Redemptoris Missio*, par. 5.

18. *Redemptoris Missio*, par. 41.

19. *Lumen Gentium*, par. 31.

20. Benedict XVI, "Message of His Holiness Pope Benedict XVI On the Occasion of the Sixth Ordinary Assembly of the International Forum of Catholic Action," https://www.vatican.va/content/benedict-xvi/en/messages/pont-messages/2012/documents/hf_ben-xvi_mes_20120810_fiac.html.

21. *Redemptoris Missio*, par. 61.

22. Augustine of Hippo, *Confessions*, trans. J. G. Pilkington (North Carolina: Oxford University Press, 2001), 109.

CHAPTER TWO: THE CENTRALITY OF THE SPIRITUAL LIFE

1. John Paul II, *Catechesi tradendae*, par. 5.

2. Francis de Sales, *Introduction to the Devout Life* (New York: Dover Publications, 2009), 41.

3. Keating, *The Heart of the Diaconate*, 7–8.

4. *Lumen Gentium*, par. 8.

5. Taken from the Prayer of Saint Michael.

6. These are also referred to as "capital sins." Pope St. Gregory the Great published the first list containing seven capital sins in the sixth century (earlier lists contain eight), and in the fourteenth century Geoffrey Chaucer popularized them in his *Canterbury Tales*.

7. John Hardon, *Pocket Catholic Dictionary* (New York: Doubleday, 1980), 60–61.

8. Aquinas, *ST*, II-II, q.35, a.1.

9. Thérèse of Lisieux, *The Story of a Soul* (New York: Dover Publications Inc., 2008), 115.

10. Francis de Sales, *The Consoling Thoughts of St. Francis de Sales*, ed. Rev. Pere Huget (Dublin: M. H. Gill and Sons, 1877), 221.

11. Jill Haak Adels, ed., *The Wisdom of the Saints* (New York: Oxford University Press, 1987), 190.

12. Josemaría Escrivá, *Christ Is Passing By* (New York: Scepter Publishers Inc., 2002), par. 75.

13. Francis de Sales, Jane de Chantal, *Letters of Spiritual Direction*, trans. Peronne Marie Thibert (New York: Paulist Press, 1988), 51.

14. Joseph M. Esper, *Saintly Solutions to Life's Common Problems* (New Hampshire: Sophia Institute Press, 2001), 287.

15. Ibid.

CHAPTER THREE: THE NECESSITY OF SURRENDER

1. Augustine, *Confessions* (New York: Penguin Books, 1960), viii.

2. Ibid.

3. Ibid.

4. Ibid., ix.

5. Thomas Aquinas, *Summa Contra Gentiles*, b.3, c.88, a.3.

6. Augustine of Hippo, *Sermons on 1 John*, Homily 7, par. 8.

7. Jean-Pierre de Caussade, *Abandonment to Divine Providence*, ed. H. Ramière (St. Louis: B. Herder Book Co., 1921), 43.

8. The Deposit of Faith (*depositum fidei*) is the body of revealed truth in the Scriptures and Tradition proposed by the Church for belief by the faithful.

9. Aquinas, *ST*, I, q.8, a.3.

10. de Caussade, *Abandonment to Divine Providence*, 6.

11. *Dei Verbum*, par. 4.

12. de Caussade, *Abandonment to Divine Providence*, 7.

13. In this work the terms envoy, emissary, ambassador, and intermediary are used synonymously. All convey, with slight nuances, one entrusted with a great mission, bearing the authority of the one who sent him.

14. de Caussade, *Abandonment to Divine Providence*, 6.

CHAPTER FOUR: THE SERVANT MYSTERIES

1. *Basic Norms for the Formation of Permanent Deacons*, par. 72.

2. Keating, *The Heart of the Diaconate*, 61–62; and "Identity and Holiness" in *The Character of the Deacon* (Mahwah, NJ: Paulist Press, 2017), 127–128.

3. John of the Cross, *The Living Flame of Love*, trans. David Lewis (New York: Cosmo Classics, 2007), 9.

4. As cited in George Cardinal Pell, "The Concept of Beauty in the Writings of Joseph Ratzinger," in *Benedict XVI and Beauty in Sacred Art and Architecture*, eds. Vincent Twomey and Janet Elaine Rutherford (Dublin: Four Courts, 2011), 25–26.

5. Augustine, *Confessions*, ed. William Mann (Oxford: Oxford University Press, 2014), 67.

6. Keating, *The Heart of the Diaconate*, 62.

7. Thomas of Celano, *The First Life of St. Francis of Assisi* (London: Christopher Stace, 2000), 96.

8. Bonaventure, *The Minor Legend*, https://www.franciscantradition.org/francis-of-assisi-early-documents/the-founder/the-legends-and-sermons-about-saint-francis-by-bonaventure-of-bagnoregio/the-minor-legend/1798-fa-ed-2-page-709.

9. Elie Wiesel, *Night* (New York: Bantam Books, 1982), 62.

10. John Vianney, Catechetical Instructions, Office of Readings, August 4.

About the Author

Deacon Dominic Cerrato is Director of the Office of the Diaconate for the Diocese of Joliet, Editor of OSV's *The Deacon* magazine, and Director of Diaconal Ministries. He has taught theology at Franciscan University of Steubenville, Duquesne University of the Holy Ghost, and Holy Apostles College and Seminary. He has nearly 30 years of experience in catechetical and pastoral ministry on both the diocesan and parish levels.

Deacon Dominic was ordained in 1995 as the first permanent deacon of the Diocese of Steubenville at the age of 35. He is a national speaker, author, and retreat master. Recently, he was appointed by Pope Francis to an international papal commission to study the question of women and the diaconate.

Deacon Dominic and his wife Judith have been married for 40 years and they have seven children and many grandchildren.

Serving deacons as they serve the Church

The Deacon is a bimonthly (6 issues/year) magazine that serves permanent deacons and deacon candidates as they serve the Church by helping them foster intimate communion with Christ the Servant.

Through a cultivation of the interior life, which leads to effective ministry, *The Deacon* contributes to the mission of the Church by making present the *totus Christus* (the "whole Christ") to the world. *The Deacon* seeks to build a community of men on fire for the diaconate through quality content that forms, informs and inspires.

Radiating joy, *The Deacon* is a trustworthy resource that accompanies deacons, deacon candidates and deacon directors as they live out, learn about and support diaconal ministry.

For more information or to start your subscription, visit **The-Deacon.com/subscribe**, or call **(800) 348-2440 and select option 2**.

Bulk and volume rates also available.